CRIME AGAINST HUMANITY

BOOKS BY THE SAME AUTHOR

1. Microbes and Diseases of Man (CBS Publishers)
2. Long Live Mao Tsetung Thought (Progressive Publications)
3. Comminform and Indian Revolution (Progressive Publications)
4. Prehistoric Man (Progressive Publications)
5. Shastrer Marxvadi Sameeksha (in Bengali, Progressive Publications)
6. Shastras (Marxist Approach)—(CBS Publishers)

CRIME AGAINST HUMANITY

DR. W.C. DEB
M.D. Ph.D.

UPPAL PUBLISHING HOUSE
NEW DELHI-110002

UPPAL PUBLISHING HOUSE
3, Ansari Road, Daryaganj, New Delhi-110002

First Published 1993
ISBN 81-85565-17-1

Printed in India
Published by B.S. Uppal for Uppal Publishing House New Delhi-110002 and Printed at R.N. Printers 1/2208. Shanti Building, Shahdara, Delhi-110032

Dedicated

to

Those who are Committed

to

'serve the people'

"Social inequalities did originate in many societies in the world in a variety of forms. But no society had ever formulated so formidable a form of inequality as the division of men on the basis of (birth in) different varnas which was devised in India. Persons of all other varnas could be punished by death, but nobody could take Brahman's life even if he had committed a hundred crimes. A Brahman could cause injury or harm to you in all possible ways but you are forbidden to do any harm to him. While you must prostrate yourself at a Brahman's feet (to touch) and take the (sacred) dust of his feet on your head, you, a Shudra must never touch him. Even water touched by a Shudra ceased to be fit for use. A Shudra had no right to (enjoy) any worldly comforts. Only the unclean occupations were for him to follow. He was denied even the right to education or knowledge which enlivens life itself. He was bound by (the tenets of) the Shastras but had no right to see for himself what these Shastras actually were. His own after-life was also very much in the hands of the Brahmans. If he did whatever the Brahman commanded him to do, his going could be good in the other world. Otherwise, there would be no salvation for him. Even a Brahman could suffer a fall in status if he accepted a (gift) present from a Shudra. Yet a Shudra was as much a human being as a Brahman. The disparity even between the slave (prisoner) and the master (captor) as it used to exist in Europe in old days, was not so heart-breaking (as that between a Shudra and a Brahman).

—Bankim Chandra Chattopadhyaya
('Samya' in Bankim Rachanavali, Vol. 2 Published by Sahitya Parishad, PP 382-83)

Preface

In the ancient past, social inequality was upheld as legitimate on the assumption that men are unequal at birth and there is nothing wrong in men being unequally placed in the society. Not only Velic Rishis but Greek Philosophers also were of the same opinion and they did not hesitate to justify gross injustice of inequality in social life. Aristotle went to the extent of remarking that there are by nature free men and slaves and that servitude is agreeable and just for the latter and the relation of the male to the female is by nature such that one is superior and the other is inferior; one dominates and the other is dominated. His assumption that men are by nature unequal in rank and that there is, therefore, a natural unequal rank of all men, however, collapsed in the face of Rousseau's assertion that according to natural law, the natural rank of all men is equal. The Declararion of Rights of Men and of the Citizen (26th August 1789) says: *Men are born and remain free and equal in rights. Social differences, therefore, can only be based on general utility.* In civilized human societies since then, inequility was no longer regarded as legitimate. Religious bigots of Hindu society are exceptions: they even now uphold legitimacy of caste inequality.

The principle of inherited inequality which provided the ideological basis of caste has been repudiated by our Constitution but it continues to govern our life. Many of the more obtrusive forms of social inequality have become obsolete in the advanced industrialised societies but in our country with outlook of deeply ingrained values supporting social hierarchy, the upper caste illiterate landowner/moneylender still enjoys a high position in the society. However, there seem to have come about an erosion in the legitimacy accorded to social inequality based on caste, particularly in cities and towns. Both economic factors as well as political ideology have played part in the decline of caste inequality. The influence of political factor is more conspicuous in our country where equalitarian ideology developed in close assoclation with nationalist movement against foreign domination especially during non-cooperation movement with participation of general masses of the people. The appeal to equalitarian values was perhaps a necessary condition for the succcss of nationalist movement and they have taken firmer roots in the post-colonial society where they are, however, coming into conflict with traditional concept of caste hierarchy and inequality. In rural areas, the old patron-client relationship is also undergoing erosion wherever revolutionary radicals are able to mobilize and organise the low caste/untouchables on class basis against class/caste oppression. Hindu fundamentalists and their patrons in the ruling class are putting up combined resistance against this development. The protagonists of caste system, with all their hypocritical postures towards the low caste/untouchables must be thoroughly exposed and repudiated through mass actions.

Although caste system is not entirely responsible for our backwardness, it acts as a very serious contributory factor. In fact, *it is the single, most important hindrance to class unity in rural areas.*

Ironically, such a system which institutionalises discrimination, hierarchy and hereditary domination is admired on the ground that it brought about assimilation of multiple tribes, races under one common umbrella of Hindu Society. Prof. Nirmal Kumar Bose (The Structure of Hindu Society) praised Brahmanism for granting different tribes freedom to continue with their own customs and rituals. But such freedom made them adherent to primitive taboos thereby keeping them totally ignorant about designs of rulers.

Three types of explanations are generally suggested about how the caste system originated (1) due to will of certain men; (2) from certain special features of the country (3) due to unique confluence of historical circumstances. In this study, the first explanation that caste originated due to the will and design of rulers, is being asserted. Those who think that the system arose out of certain special features tend to ignore the history of tyranny of the conquering tribe over the multiple less vigorous smaller tribes who had been the local inhabitants. W.W. Hunter (Annals of Rural Bengal) adduced evidences testifying that the invading Aryans perpetrated most crude forms of tyranny against the pre-Aryan autochthones. Even Ashoka, regarded as the ideal ruler did not hesitate to evict 150,000 pre-Aryans of Kalinga, from their native land; deported and employed them in far away Gangetic belt in the task of clearing forests for the benefit of the Aryan settlers there! They were generously assimilated in Hindu society as slaves or Shudras. Chandals who reportedly cooperated with Aryan Rama in his battle with 'Rakshashas' but were later uprooted by his descendents and they had to settle in South India and Madhya Pradesh as displaced persons or refugees! They could not be assimilated in caste structure and had to remain as Untouchables or Outcasts!

Dr. W.C. Deb

A-42, Chittaranjan Park.
New Delhi—110019

Introduction

"The kings of antiquity, who were industriously devoted to the duties of their office, spent most of their care on the division of their subjects into different classes and orders, which they tried to preserve from intermixture and disorder. Therefore, they forbade people of different classes to have intercourse with each other and laid upon each class a particular kind of work or art and handicraft. They did not allow anybody to transgress the limits of his class, and even punished those who would not be content with their class."

—AL BIRUNI.*

Explaining the origin of caste system of India, he made the above comment. In ancient India, the strategy of 'Divide and Rule' seems to have found expression in the form of caste or 'Varna system.

Smriti Shastras as well as Kautilya's Arthashastra dealt with the conception of Kingship in ancient India and emphasised that Kingship is essential for social order. It is significant that 'Chaturvarnya' or the four Varna division of the society had been supported by all kings including even some Buddhist kings. Those kings were not all Aryans; even some who claimed descent

*According to Suniti Kumar Chatterji, Al-Biruni was the greatest of all indologists.

from pre-Aryan 'Naga's or' Aswathwama's of Mahabharata or some monkey-king of Ramayana were also patrons of the varna or caste system.

During the initial stage of varna-division, Khatriyas were at the top of hierarchy and by the time of Upanishads, division of the society into four varnas became well established with the kings or Kshatriyas as the ruling class (physical power) and the Brahmans (spiritual force) living under their direct patronage. Kshatriyas and Brahmans were opposed to Vaisyas; for the latter the Lord of creatures has made over only the cattle, to the former all the creatures (Manu, IX, 327). And Shudras are devoid of any direct relation to religion; their sole task is to serve the other castes without envy. (Manu Samhita, I, 88-91). There had been solidarity of Kshatriyas and Brahmans vis-a-vis the rest. In M.S. (IX, 322), Kshatriya and Brahman can not prosper separately but only in close association. The pair Brahma-Kshatriya opposed itself, not so much to the sole Vaishya, but rather to all the rest. There are many other passages illustrating the necessary solidarity, distinction and hierarchy of the functions of Brahmans and Kshatriyas. For example, Brahman seems to put himself beyond the authority of the king: "Here is your king, O people; Soma is the king of us, Brahmans." (Sat. Br. V, 3, 3, 12); or "the priest makes the king weaker than himself and thus he (the king) will be stronger than his enemies". (Sat Br. V, 8, 9, 15). Commenting on the tussle between the two, Pandit Nilkanta Shastri (Cultural Heritage of India, Vol. II, p. 485) said: "Traces are not altogether wanting that at some stage, superiority of the 'imperium' was clearly asserted and 'Brahma' had definitely to accept a lower place. Soon, however, the balance tilted in favour of the spiritual power and the change appeared to be based on bold trick of etymology by which name 'Purohita (placed before) of the spiritual office is made to gain precedence for it". 'Baudhayana Sutra' lays down that the king should choose a person of high ability as his purohita and they obey his behests. And Kautilya compares the relation of the king to the purohita to that of the pupil to his teacher, the son to the father and the servant to the master. Thus, *there was a contradiction as well as unity between the two*. The unity was against the other two varnas. Rig Veda (V, 50, 8) clearly states that the security of the Group depended on the Coorperation of physical force (Kshatra) and spiritual power (Brahma).

The division of society into four varnas was accorded religious sanction, the significance of which is best described by Rabindranath Tagore (Kalantar): "There is a need for the work of a 'Faras' (Servant) but for him the work is not to his linking. Under the circumstances, it is very insulting to be forced or compelled to work as a servant. India solved this problem by making profession division hereditory. If by Government ordinance it was done, there would have been dis-grace of slavery and attempts to rebel would not have stopped. It became permanent by rellgious sanction. In our country, *by inclusion of profession division within religious regulations such discontentment and the root of attempt at 'Viplab' (revolution) had been demolished*". The divine origin of 'Varna' is an obvious myth but the working people particularly those of lower castes in rural areas have accepted it as truth!

The duties and rights of four 'Varnas' have been specified in detail in 'Manu-Samhita'—the 'Dharmashastra'. In fact, Manu's rules have governed the conduct of the Hindu population since antiquity. Of all kinds of social inequalities prevalent in the world, the Varna or caste system represents the most discriminatory one. The privileges for the Brahmans are innumerable. When all other people are punishable by death sentence; the Brahman can never be executed even for the worst of all crimes; he can only be banished from the kingdom for such a crime. The Brahman can do harm to you but you, the non-Brahmans can never do any harm to him. All non-Brahmans are to lay prostrate at the feet of the Brahman; the Shudra is untouchable, he is not to touch the feet even! A Shudra is not entitled to any kind of happiness; he has to perform only abdominable deeds. He is bound by the Shastras but he has not the right to see the Shastras; not only his present life but his after-life also is in the hands of Brahmans! About Shudras, Manu Samhita (VIII, 414-416) clearly defines the position: "Shudra is not liberated from slavery even if he is released by his master or owner. To work as a slave is natural for him; so who can liberate him from slavery? One who is owned after victory in warfare; the devoted slave i.e. the one who accepts slavery for food; one who is the son of a maid servant; one who has been bought by paying money; one who is adopted i.e. who has been gifted by another; one who is sentenced to slavery for some crimes—these are the *seven kinds of slaves recognised by the Shastras*".

About 'Chandals, Manu's specific directions (Sloka-X, 51-52) were: "Chandala and Swapach should be allowed living space outside the village and they must be made devoid of utensils. Fowls and asses are their only wealth. They have to wear clothing of dead bodies, to eat in a broken plate, and in the night time, their movement is prohibited inside the village. During day time, they must bear a mark conferred by the king and in that condition only they can move, and they should remove unclaim-dead bodies from village".

In modern India, the last privilege has been denied to them! Such a system is supported not only by the religious bodies but also the overwhelming majority among upper caste elites on the the plea that such a system was necessary in ancient India!

Contents

Preface vii

Introduction x

1. What is Caste? 1
2. Ideological Basis of Caste System 10
3. Theories on the Origin of Caste System 15
4. Historical Development of Caste System 23
5. Caste and Class 47
6. Political and Social Consequences of Caste System 53
7. Magnitude of the Caste Problem 67
8. Atrocities on Scheduled Castes and Scheduled Tribes 81
9. Caste and Slavery 95
10. Caste and Politics 102
11. Backwardness and Caste 118
12. Government Welfare Measures 140
13. Conclusion 169

1

What is Caste ?

Caste is the prototype of rigid social inequality. It is both a form of social organisation and a system of values. As a form of social organisation it is marked by a division of the society into groups which are ranked in an elaborate hierarchy. As a system of value it is characterised by the legitimacy it accords to social inequality and the importance given to the ideas of purity and pollution. The original 'Varna' or colour has changed to 'Jati' (literally meaning birth) or Caste. The former was based on colour of the skin or 'guna-karma' (character-profession) and the latter on birth. The word 'casta' signified breed, race or rank. The first use of the word (caste) dates from 1563 A.D. when Gracia de Orta wrote: "No one changes from his father's trades and all those of the same caste (casta) of shoe-makers are the same" (Hutton). The word seems to have been used in the sense of race by Spaniards. In India, the Portugese Council of Goa have applied it; and since the beginning of 17th century the word is being used in the Indian sense of 'Jati'.

The word 'varna' has been taken by Jurists, Anthropologists and Indologists to mean 'class'. However, the word 'varna' means class without any connotation of rank while in the 'Chaturvarnya' system the idea of rank both social and religious, predominates.

The word 'varna' represents the theory of the caste structure; and it may be taken to be equivalent to 'group'. 'Jati' represents the functional aspect of caste system. 'Varna' stands for ritual rank; jati for social status. Dharma-Shastras refers to 'Varna' as the theory of caste system.

Endogamy was not a characteristic of varna-system. Many Brahman rishis had Kshatriya wives e.g. Agasthya's Lopamudra, Hrishyashringa's Santa, Jamadagni's Renuka. After extermination of Kshatriya race (males) by Parasurama, Kshatriya widows were all impregnated, if not marrried by Brahmans. Brahman daughter Devayani married Kshatriya king Yajati. In caste system (jati), along with heredity strict *endogamy* is enforced. However, there is no doubt that in Vedic period there had been no endogamy. According to Bankim Chandra Chattopadhyaya, the three dwija varnas had *interdining* also. In the caste system, now prevalent in rural areas, interdining is strictly prohibited.

Caste is an important reflection of the actual *relation of production*, particularly at the time of its introduction.

Definition of Caste

Risley: "A collection of families or groups of families bearing a common name, claiming as common descent from a mythical ancestor human or divine, professsing to follow the same hereditory calling and regarded by those who are competent to give an opinion as forming a single homogeneous community".

Ketkar: "A social group having two characteristics: (1) membership is confined to those who are born of members, and includes all persons so born; (2) members are forbidden by inexorable social laws to marry outside the group."

According to Hutton (Caste in India), "Kayasthas. ranking next to Brahmans in Bengal are probably really an occupational caste in origin and as writer may have been recruited from more than one varna". Regarding 'Exterior Castes' he, as Census Commissioner of 1931 instructed: "I have explained depressed castes as castes, contact with whom entails purifcation on the part of high caste Hindus. It is not intended that the term should have reference to occupation as such but to those castes which by reason of their traditional position in Hindu society are denied access to temples, for instance, or have to use separate wells or are not allowed to sit inside a school house but to remain outside or which suffer from similar disabilities".

Manusamhita says that all jatis are derived through marriages of people of different varnas. But the rules of 'Anuloma' (bride of lower varna) and 'Pratiloma' (bride of higher varna) marriages contradict Manu's attempt to derive castes from intermarriage of varnas; because, if a child belonged to the varna of his father such a large number of castes could not come into existence from the original four varnas. Manu's system had been modified to a great extent. Amongst the Shudras, a sub-group arose and it was made of certain castes (?) whose touch (even their shadow) was held to be polluting and that was the rank of 'Untouchables'. Even though there are innumerable castes and sub-castes in modern India. there are only three important castes: Brahmans, Shudras and Untouchables, especielly in Bengal and South India.

The transition of the society from varna to jati (caste) seems to be associated with an extraordinary theoretical development taking place around the beginning of the Christian era when the influence of Buddhism and Jainism popularised the idea of renunciation. At that time, having begun in the sects of renouncers, vegetarianism and 'Ahimsa' forced themselves on Hindu society. This is evident in the slokas of Manu-Samhita. Meat retains all its values in offerings to the ancestors and the link between sacrifice and consumption of meat is stressed. But in verse 53, abstention from meat is said to be equivalent to hundred horse-sacrifices.. It is also said that 'to kill in sacrifice is not to kill, whereas in verses 44 and 45 'Ahimsa' is praised! Obviously, under the pressure of the ideology of 'Ahimsa' in particular, Brahmans brought about basic changes in the social structure; varna was changed to jati and both heredity and endogamy were made obligatory.

From anthropological point of view, the caste is defined as a circle beyond which nobody is allowed to marry. Thus caste or subcaste is an endogamous social group based on blood bond. A clan is defined as a group of families, all tracing their descent to a distant common ancestor, either male or female. Such a clan is always exogamous and is used as a surname. The counterpart of clan is 'gotra'. A caste is an extension of the group principle as manifested in the joint family. All members of a particular caste are related by blood or marriage. The caste is inclusive of the clan, which, in turn, includes several joint families; while the latter two are exogamous, the caste is strictly endogamous. Even in modern times, an elite, including those belonging to parliamentary communist parties do not ordinarily want to marry their daughters to a boy outside their own castes. Among some communities, the caste ties are stronger than regional or linguistic considerations. This is marked among Marwaris and people of Bihar.

According to Dr. Ambedkar, "Caste system is not merely division of labour. It is also a division of labourers. It is a hierarchy in which the division of labourers is gradad one above the other. *Caste system embodied the arrogance and selfishness of a perverse section of Hindus* who were superior enough in social status to set a fashion and who had authority to force it on their inferiors."

The words 'castes' and 'sub-castes' represent larger and single collections of endogamous groups respectively. The *subcastes*, *however, are not products of fission of a caste*; rather they seem to be of independent and different origins.

With the Shudra caste, the number of Untouchables increases as one goes from the north to the south of the country. The difference between ranks of higher and lower castes is manifested by the physical distance in the form of different habitation areas. In South India the distance at which a man of a particular caste had to stand in order to speak to a Brahman was fixed in yards. This distance placed each caste in a precise ranking system.

Most of the castes are within the 200,000 limit in number. The Marathas of Maharastra, however, number in millions. The Brahmans make up about 9% of the population in Maharastra; Marathas 30%, Vaishyas 5% and Shudras 56% of which about 9% belong to the scheduled castes or Untouchables. In Tamilandu, there is no Kshatriya, a very small number of Vaishyas so that the percentage of Shudras is far more than in Maharastra.

The permanence of caste division was ensured by its being made hereditory; the primitive taboo of eating together became caste law and this in turn made it necessary to define marriage limits, leading to elaborate rules of endogamy and exogamy. The evolution of caste society was a very slow process. The basis and continuance of the Caste System depended not on the basic four fold division but on the vast network of subcastes, which was intimately connected with occupation. Eventually, the sub-caste came to assume more relevance for the working of Hindu society than the main castes, since the functioning of the society was mainly dependent on sub-caste relationship and adjustments, the varnas remaining an overall theoretical framework, the Varna remaining an overall framework. Sub-Caste relationships were based on specialization of work and economic interdependence.

The original caste-hierarchy is no longer tenable. During the last five centuries in Uttar Pradesh and West Bengal the

'Kayasthas' have been the most powerful caste. About Kayasthas, one is not certain about their status in the original 4 varnas. They are neither Brahmans nor Khsatriyas. According to Bankim Chandra Chattopadhyayay, kayasthas are 'Varna-Sankar' due to admixture of Aryan and non-Aryan races. In Rajputana, Brahmans are third after Rajputs (non-Aryan Khsatriyas) and Banias; in Maharashtra, Marathas have been the ruling race etc. In Andhra Pradesh, Reddis and Kammas are the most dominant.

The caste system has a double aspect. Much of the diversity of the Indian social life is due to caste system which jealously guard and conserve its peculiar mores; damns small cultural streams within its narrow limits and act as a barrier to the free intercourse and cultural assimilation. The other aspect is that caste's function towards other groups is one of negative aloofness but towards its own members, it is almost a social universe. As a result, caste acts as the *greatest impediment in class unity* amongst the rural people.

New jatis were formed either by professional groups taking on a jati status or else by tribes being incorporated as jatis. Professional groups of administrators and traders also emerged as new castes; Kayasthas and Khatri. Village officials with designations such as 'Mahattara', Pathakila' and 'Gavumda', mentioned in the inscriptions of the medieval period occur today as the castes of Mehta, Patel or Patil and Gaudd. (R.S. Sharma-'Social Changes in Early Medieval India'). Tribes converted into castes are Abhira, Kirata. Originally they were dvija but they were reduced to Shudra. Dharmasasra mentions the professional groups which became castes: Ayaskara (Blacksmith), Kuloka (Potter), Gopa (Herdsmen), Tantuvaya (Weaver) and Tailika (Oilmen).

Caste Division in Bengal

'Brihad-dharma' and 'Brahma-Vaivarta' Puranas contain elaborate description about different castes. The former recommends eating of fish and meat for Brahmans and mentions about 36 sub-castes among Shudras; obviously this Purana represents the then social conditions of Bengal. It is also noteworthy that there is no mention about difference between Kshatriya and Vaisya; and Shudras are divided into two categories 'good' and 'bad'. Outside Bengal, such caste division does not exist.

From anthropological point of view, upper caste Brahmans were probably 'Alpine' and they were immigrents to Bengal; whereas the local autochthones were pre-Dravidian 'Ausral'. According to Atul Sur, in ancient Bengal, there had been rather indistinct difference between Brahmans and other upper caste Hindus. He opined that the surnames used by modern non-Brahman upper Caste Hindus such as Ghosh, Basu, Mitra, Gupta, Pal, Sen, Chandra etc. were used by the then Brahmans! However. it would be not proper to determine the caste on the basis of surnames. The people of Bengal have been described as 'Asura' in 'Manjusri-kalpa', 'Mahabharata' and 'Haribansa'; and are believed to be descendants of Asura King Vali and Queen Sudeshna. 'Matsya' and 'Vayu' Puranas aiso hold that descendants of Asura King Vali are the creators of four 'Varnas'. Thus, from ethnological consideration, people of ancient Bengal had little or no blood of 'Nordic' Aryan race. Probably, for this reason, even today conservativc Brahmans of North India hesitate to marry their daughter to a Bengali Brahman bridegroom.

Biroja Sankar Guha has shown that the skull-shape of the people of Eastern India is round, while that of people of north India is oblong-elliptical. He also pointed out the difference between Brahmans, Kayasthas and Pods in shape of skull, nose and height (1.68 m., 1.67 m. and 1.628 m. respectively). It is generally recognised that Bengalis are ethnically 'Sankara's. The widespread admixture was probably effected through Anuloma and Pratiloma marriages. *During the rule of Pala Kings, most of the low caste Hindu population became Buddhists, but there occurred remergence of 'Chaturvarna' culture under the patronage of Sen kings* who were migrants to Bengal from Karnataka.

The original [(Moulik) Brahmans of Bengal had their own individual gotras or ancestry. Since the 8th century, Brahmans from outside Bengal began to migrate to Bengal.

They came from Kroranchi, Tarkari (near Sravasti of U.P.) Matsyabas, Kuntir, Chandwar (District of Etawa), Hastipada, Muktabastu, even Lal (Gujarat). Sen Kings were conservative Hindus and they introduced the tradition of conferring the 'Kulin' status to some Brahmans. According to some authors, the 'Kulin' status was extended to even the non-Brahman upper castes such as Vaidya, Kayastha and Sat-Shudra. The status of 'kulin' was accorded on the basis of 'Guna' (qualities); never was it hereditary. Those who possessed 9 qualities such as mannerliness, modesty, knowledge, fame, pilgrimage, dedication, satiety, meditation and gift were awarded the kulin status. Those having 8 qualities were 'Siddhasrotriya'. This system is prevalent among the 'Rarhi' Brahmans. 'Barendra' Brahmans are divided into three categories: Kulin, Srotriya and Kap (Bansaja). Bhanga-Kulins are Kap or Bansaja.

It is generally agreed that Maharaja Adisur brought five Brahmans from Kanauj. After their return from Bengal, they were not accepted by the society because they became polluted by the climatic environment of Bengal. Such was the then society! So they came back to Bengal and along with them came five Kayasthas as servants (to carry footwear and umbrella). The Brahmans were of 5 different 'gotra's—Sandilya, Kashyap, Batsya, Bhardwaj and Savarna. According to 'Rarhi' Pundits the number of Brahmans rose to 59 during the reign of Kshitisur who divided them into 3 categories—Kulin, gauna-kulin and Srotriya. 'Barendra' Brahmans were made 'kulin' by Ballalsen. There is no doubt that the *system of Kulin was the result of ruler's whim only*. Currently Bengali Hindu society has got five broad divisions—Brahman, Vaidya, Kayastha, Navasakh and other castes. The castes from whom Brahmans accept water are included in Navasakh—they are Tili, Tanti (weaver). Malakar (gardener), Sadgop, Napit (barber), Barni, Kamar (blacksmith), Kumar (potter), Gandhavanik and Modak (sweets maker). *Suvarnavaniks were downgraded by Ballalsen.* It is said that Ballavananda, the 'sresthi' chief of that age refused to lend money to the king and in retaliation, they were made out-castes from the Navasakh group. Following this incident, the number of Vaisyas among Bengalis dwindled. Tili and Suri began to act as merchants and moneylenders, *The 'Sadhu' word in Sanskrit means Vanik or trader and probably Sau, Saha, Shah are nothing but distortions of 'Sadhu'.*

Apparent absence of caste oppression in Bengal is indicative of the undisputed domination of the upper caste 'bhadralok's. Even in villages. the bargadars mostly belonging to low castes/ Untouchables have gained during the left front government and they all became part of the ruling political party. Moreover the radical communist revolutionaries are in complete disarray organisationally and consequently unlike in Bihar, the hegemony of the upper caste exploiters is yet to be challanged. The low caste/untouchable poor peasants and landless agricultural labourers are not organised to fight against economic exploitation and caste oppression.

2

Ideological Basis of Caste System

A Marathi poet (Gobindraj) describes in one of his poems that Hindu caste system makes a man"*bow his head to the kicks from above, and who himself simultaneously gives a kick below, never thinking to resist the one or to refrain from the other*". In Hinduism truth, 'ahimsa' and tolerance are taught but there is *little concern for justice in social life*. Thus, ranking or hierarchy of caste system not only perpetuates inequality and discrimination; *it also engenders contempt for the downtrodden.* Even the low caste Hindu despises another Hindu belonging to the caste lower than his. He only desires to rise in social status so that he can kick more people below!

Taittiriya-Samhita (2.5.10) clearly states: "*One of the chief purpose of sacrifice was to make the other castes obedient to Kshtriya varna*". Obviously, caste division was designed to make the subjects subservient to King.

The doctrines of 'Karma' and 'Rebirth' had been the justification of miseries in the present life; and Sankhya philosophy emphasises that wordly life is full of miseries. According to the doctrine of 'Karma', every act of man has a plus or minus value. At death, if the plus value is more than the minus value, that individual would be born either in heaven or on earth in a status better than the one enjoyed by him now. But if the balance is on the minus side, then he goes to hell or is born on earth in a lower status, or as a beast or plant until the minus balance is exhausted! The very fact that one is born means that he is reborn until one is able to attain 'liberation' or 'Moksh'. This is the doctrine of rebirth.

These doctrines must have helped to palliate the inequality and other injustices inherent in the caste system but the question is whether these ideas were grafted on to the system in the course of its development or the underlying philosophy itself was propounded, as a design to justify the system. Analysis of these two doctrines in the context of the philosophy of 'Brahma' leads to the conclusion that philosophies of 'Sankhya' and 'Vedanta' (which were described as erroneous by Pandit Iswar Chandra Vidyasagar) were at the basis of 'Karma' and 'Rebirth' doctrines. Even though, theoretically it is possible for all members of caste-divided socity to achieve a plus balance of some sort and thus raise traditionalism to be the highest moral conduct, there is no doubt that some social status is more conducive to accumulation of plus points easily than some others. It is taught by Shastras that one has to bear one's earthly lot; if sad, without rancour; if good, without pride and in that case would the gates of release (from rebirth) be opened. Thus, the basic assumption is that birth itself is the worst mis-fortune. This reactionary philosophy has been repudiated by Rabindranath Tagore in his poem: "I do not want to die in this beautiful world". Bertrand Russel (Unpopular Essays) pointed out: One of the persistant delusion of mankind is that some sections of human race are morally better or worse than others". This belief has different forms, none of which has any rational basis. Hindu caste system is one such form having no rational basis. He also described "Extermination of conquered race is a religious duty (Old Testament)" as a harmful belief. The Vedic Aryans did not exterminate but made them slaves or Shudras. The pre-Aryan local autochthones, commonly described as non-Aryan or Dravidian are all clustered in the lowest Shudra caste or declared as Untouchables; and they all were of the conquered raees or tribes.

Religious and quasi-religious beliefs and practices are based on the principles of magic, mana, taboo and other ideas which had been prevalent in the primitive human society. In the chapter titled 'Primitive Thought' of 'A Short History of the World', H.G. Wells writes: "Systematic thought is apparently a comparatively late development in human experience, it has not played any great part in human life until within 3000 years. Most of the world still lives by imagination and passion. Probably, the earlist human societies, in the opening stages of human story were small family groups. But before this could happen a certain restraint upon the primitive egotism of the individual had to be established...Human Social life grew up out of the reaction between the crude instinct of the young to go off and pair by themselves as they grow up, on the one hand, and the danger and disadvantages of isolation on the other. *Much of the customary laws of savages, the Taboo's can be ascribed to such a mental attachment of the needs of the primitive human animal to a developing sociol life* . . . He believed and tried in a thousand charms, incantations and omens to determine the desirable results in hunting games. Quite early in the tribe, older steadier minds sharing fears, sharing imaginations but a little more forceful than others must have asserted themselves to advise, to prescribe, to command. This they declared propitious, and that imperative, this an omen of good and that an omen of evil. *The expert in Fetish, the Medicine Man, was the first priest.* He exhorted, he interpreted dreams, he warned, he performed the complicated hocus pocus that brought luck or averted calamity". In our country, taboos of primitive man persist not only amongst the illitetate rural folk but also among the majority of urban elites. The ideology of priests of barbaric and early stage civilization (Vedic age) were basically same as that of primitive religion during savagery. Charms, incantations and omens are still believed by Hindu population vitiated by the caste system. Old men's fear of young men going off and pairing by themselves had been mitigated by the institution of the tradition of marriage through parental negotiation and choice. It appearr that *prohibition of intercaste marriage in based on this primitive fear of the old.* Taboos of certain foods, the beliefs that food may be infected with dangerous soul-matter of the stranger and that there may be magical effects of the food on the consumer were quite strong amongst the primitives. It was also believed that by cooking, the food is cooked with the 'Mana' of the cook. Thus, it is quite possible that *such primitive ideas about food is at the root of prohibition of inter-dining.* There are evidences to the effect that primitive people had the belief that *foods have the power to transmit qualities.* Primitive ideas of pollution, ablution, purification by bath in holy water are still pre-valent among Hindus, in general. Ideas of exclusive family, ancestor worship and sacramental meals are also possible factors contributing to the emergence and development of caste system.

In sum, it may be stated that even if the origin was only in the form of tribal exclusiveness with primitive ideas of purity and impurity, *the later development into a hierarchial rigid institution was certainly a deliberate action on the part of exploiting class to keep the manual labourers under subjugation* and such institution was proclaimed to be of divine origin so that the common man would accept it without examination and protest. The materialistic philosophers (Charvak) who opposed it and exposed the evil design were liquidated by force of arms (Mahabharata). Dr. Ambedkar held that "*the caste system was a legal system maintained at the point of bayonet.* If it had survived, it was due to prevention of the masses from the possession of arms, denying to the masses the right to education and depriving the masses of the right to property. *The caste system was an imposition by the ruling class over the servile classes*". According to him, classes had become caste through initiation and exocommunication.

Buddhism also had its own contribution to make to the development of caste system. The 'Karma' doctrine of the belief in transmigration of soul is the bedrock of Buddhist philosophy. The caste system was rationalised by such doctrine because it creates a belief in its equity even among those who were its wrost victims. The doctrine of Ahimsa, so popular among the cattle-raising Vaishyas who all supported Budhism provided reason for the subjugation and humiliation of food-gathering communities. *The Asokan edicts contain injunctions against hunting and fishing.* Moreover, Buddhist texts look down upon animal killing as much as Hindu texts do. Like Brahmanism, Buddhism also contributed to the denigration of land-cultivating peasants. Manu Samhita (X, 84) condemns land cultivation for the injury that the plough causes living creatures present in the soil. I't-sing records that the *Buddha forbade monks from engaging in land cultivation because this involved "destroying lives by ploughing* and watering fields"!!

Thus it would not be correct to suppose that caste ideology had been exclusively Brahmanical in its development. However, there is no doubt that Brahmanism had been the initiator and Brahmans played the crucial role.

It must be noted that the word Varna or Jati never appear in Asoka's texts; obedience to the Varna rules does not form a part of the 'Dharma' that Asoka propagated. Obviously Bhddhism questioned the legitimacy of the Varna-division inherited from the Vedic texts.

3

Theories on the Origin of Caste System

Precisely when the caste system originated, it is difficult to establish but there is no doubt that the institution of caste arose as an expedient of administration executed by the ruling class. Prof. Benoy Kumar Sarkar (Cultural Heritage of India. Vol. II, p. 409) writes: "*Varnasram though an ethnico-economic and socio-pedagogic term is fundamentally a political concept*". Iravati Karve also stated (Economic weekly, Special Number, July 1958): "*The four rank system was creation of the ruling class* which originally had a three rank system in which, whatever the differences of rank, all people had the right to certain rituals and sacraments from birth to death". Prof. K.M. Sen (Hinduism, p. 27-28) commented: "As conquerors, however, they must have felt more powerful. and as strong believers in the Vedic religion, with its elaborate pantheon, they may have thought themselves right-minded. Whatever the truth, the resultant plural society with different communities, different religious beliefs, different attitudes to life, and different occupations, *the conquerors who formed most of the new upper classes produced a rigid caste structure*. *In all probability, some sort ofcaste divisions already existed when Aryans arrived and the Aryans made most of it*". D.D. Kosambi also held similar opinion. He writes: (Bhagawan Buddha) "*Even before Vedic age in the country of seven rivers and central India, alongwith cult of nonviolence, the cult of caste was also present.* (Bhagawan Buddha). As evidence he mentions that the killing of Vritrasura (non-Aryan) by Indra (Aryan) is described in the Mahabharata as a sin of killing a Brahman; Sukracharya the 'guru' (teacher) of non-Aryans was the son of Bhrigu whose other sons included Parasuram, the Brahman who exterminated Kshatriyas. The non-Aryan king of Lanka-Ravana is also decribed as a Brahman!

Stuart Piggot (Prehistoric India) also suggested that Harappa civilization had a strongly theocratic tinge and the stratification of the then society suggests that *a caste pattern may have existed at that time.* Ronald Segal (Crisis of India) writes: "When the existence of housing quarters for workmen of special trades very near the location of their quarters is considered alongside the static street plan of the cities throughout a thousand years, *the possibility that caste structure, occupational and hereditory in basis had already taken shape before the arrival of the Aryans can not be easily dismissed as unreal*". Whether the Aryans, in fact, did adopt the institution of caste from the culture they conquered or originated themselves can not be established but there is no doubt that they promoted it as a method of pervasive control over the discontent against exploitation and oppression of the actual producers of wealth. The Aryan priests established their supremacy in the caste structure by adopting strict rules for each caste.

Pargiter (Archive Orient Dini, IV, p. 2, August 1932) also adduced evidence that Brahman families are of pre-Vedic origin, and Madhyadesh kings were their own priests. In earliest times there was no Brahman priests.

In view of the above facts, we have to look for the origin of caste in the priests, of presumably pre-Aryan Dravidian race. The existence of public baths with steps and broken earthenware glasses in large number both at Harappa and Mahenjo-daro indicates that the taboo of untouchability and purification by bath in holywater had been in practice. The fact that largest number of Untouchables are in South India inhabited by pre-Aryans or Dravidians is strongly suggestive of *pre-Aryan origin of untouchability*. The contest between Vashista and Vishwamitra and ultimately the latter's formal renunciation of Kshtriya way seem to represent the final ascendancy of pre-Aryan religion. Slater (Dravidian element in Indian Culture) suggests that caste arose in India before Aryan invasion, as a result of occupation being hereditary and marriages being arranged by parents.

In ancient times, ideas about soul stuff or life matter and of necessity of protecting it by the observance of taboo were, common and our caste system is undoubtedly based on ideas of soul, mana, and magic. The Sanskrit literature has always described magic as "Asur-Vidya" and the 4th Vedas-Atharva Veda which is primarily concerned with magic-mantras is believed to be of non-Aryan composition. However, it is true that Rig Vedic Aryans introduced the principle of social precedence into a society already divided into groups isolated by taboos.

Divergent views have been expressed as to the process by which the unique Hindu caste system had evolved. Senart, the noted French Orientalist thought that the distribution of Aryans over large areas resulted in multiplication of groups, contact with the local non-Aryan inhabitants encouraged pride of blood; the idea of ceremonial purity led to the employment of the latter in occupations involving manual labour and all these conditions gave rise to family worship and caste exclusiveness. He pointed out that the *Aryan institutions of family, gens and tribe corresponded respectively to the family, the gotra and the caste.*

Slater, a professor of economics in the University of Madras promulgated, probably for the first time that *caste is a Dravidian institution.* He argued that they (Dravidians) had behind them the tradition of magic and priestcraft which helped the acquisition of power and influence. The association of magical practices and religious ceremonies with the work of the craft helped in the building up of caste solidarity. The tropical climate leads to early sexual maturity and that again to marriages of boys who are still immature in other respects. Naturally in these circumstances it is his father who selects the bride for him and it is very natural that he selects the bride from the family of men who follow the same craft. As a result marriage outside the craft became one of the things which were not done and, therefore, reprehensible. In respect of the Dravidian origin of Brahman Caste, he advanced 4 arguments: (1) The Brahmans have a tradition of descent from an ancestry different from that of commonality (2) The carriers of the heliolithic culture claimed divinity, and it is also the traditional Brahman theory that every Brahman is a God. (3) if Brahma is a solar deity the whole Brahman caste is even more closely associated with sun worship, and (4) the carriers of the heliolithic culture brought from Egypt a knowledge of arts of spinning and weaving as well as agriculture, and the distinguishing mark of the Brahmans is the sacred cotton cord worn by him inside all other clothing". The last evidence, says Slater "appears to be a very clear indication that the Brahman ascendancy has one of its roots in the dcscent of the Brahman from the foreigners who earned the gratitude and homage of the population of India by teaching them to spin and weave".

In favour of Dravidian origin of caste system, Dr. Hutton (caste in India) also advanced the argument that the existence among the Brahui tribe of Beluchistan of a strong preference to endogamy is decidedly suggestive of the caste system. He gives thc following explanations about the origin of caste: "The sentiments and beliefs on which caste is presumably based, go back to the totemistic Proto-Australoid and to the Austro-Asiatic inhabitant of pre-Dravidian India and we may conceive of their becoming effective on contact with Dravidian-speaking strangers bringing new crafts from the west. Hence would arise local tabus, against centain crafts and certain persons, tabus tending to become tribal and to erect rigid division between communities. Even in early Vedic literature, different words appear for identical occupations. With culturally superior strangers, hypergamy must almost certainly arise, and if there came a foreign priest-hood with the ancient sciences of South-West Asia, the belief in their magical powers would make them most heavily tabued of all".

They hypothesised that the food or other contacts of strangers is itself regarded as dangerous owing to a supposed infection with the dangerous 'mana (mind) or soul matter. The differentiation between cooked and uncooked food as a vehicle for pollution is traceable to the view of infection, by the act of cooking, of the food cooked with the 'mana' of the cook. However. Hutton argues: not that caste in its present form is a pre-Aryan development but that without these pre-Aryan ingredients "the development of caste would not and could not have taken place". The pre-Aryan rather pre-Dravidian origin of food and other tabus has been emphasised by other authors like Oldengerg, Rice and Gait. Hutton held that *the motive spring of caste is contained in the primitive 'mana' philosophy.*

D.D. Kosambi's idea about the origin of caste system is as follows: "We can get a rather faint glimpse of the four-caste system in its most remote (pre-Buddhistic) orlgin and it is, as far as can be seen, pre-Aryan, probably associated with the ancient civilization of Mohenjo-Daro and the Indus Valley, and with its destruction in or about the second millennium B.C. by the Aryans. It may reasonably be conjectured, the conquering warriors swept away a civilization which had accurate weights and good cities but no weapons to speak of. After years, probably centuries, of a fearfully hungry existence in the forests, *one clan of the conquered becomes the priest caste of the conquerors: the Bhargava Brahmans. The conquerors become the*

Kashtriya caste, being warriors. The traders are present from older times, and the rest of the population sinks to a regularised slavery but without large scale trading in human beings as in the west, being the Shudra Caste. *The prohibition against a Shudra learning the trade of weapons and against his education in the Sanskrit language, therefore, is a precautionary or a police measure against helots*". (History and Society). Thus, according to him, of the four castes, only the *Kshatriyas are Aryans*; *Brahmans, Vaishyas and Shudras are all pre-Aryans.* Probably for this reason, Viswamitra is regarded by him as the true Aryan.

Discussing the probable origin of Brahman, D.D. Kosambi pointed out: "Vashista came of the human representative of a pre-Aryan mother goddess and as such no father. Going over to the patri-archal system, Aryans required some respectable father and at the same time a denial of non-Aryan mother. So Vashista was said to be born in a jar (womb). Agasthya was also similarly born in a jar! The jar undoubtedly represents the womb and thereby the mother Goddess. Vishwamitra is the only genuine Aryan of the lot. The adoption of such jar-born seers into the high Aryan priesthood was a fundamental innovation. By such recombination of Aryan and auto-chthones, new class of specialists developed which would eventuathly claim monopoly of all Aryan rituals of the Brahman caste".

According to Ambedkar's theory of the origin of untouchability the ancestors of Untouchables were what is called "Broken Men", the remnants of class or tribes who had been defeated in the intertribe conflicts and so forced to live on the outskirts of villages inhabited by the conquering tribes. The "Broken Men" adopted Buddhism and had to continue to live outside the villages and they performed menial jobs and some watch and ward duties. *They also continued to eat beef which the Hindus had given up to be one better than Buddhists.* As a result, they finally came to be looked upon as Untouchable."

Hutton (Caste in India), on the other hand writes: "Probably enough emphasis has not been laid on the geographical aspect of the situation. Many roads of migration have led into India and have ended there. So there is accumulation of large number of societies of very different levels of culture and very varying customs in an area in which they have neither been mutually inacessible nor without some measure of individual isolation. The mere necessity of finding a modus vivendi on the part of a number of different cultures has probably played not an unimportant part among the various factors that have combined to cause the caste system to develop". According to W.W. Hunter (Annals of Rural Bengal), *the people of ancient India were divided into two principal groups; upper caste Aryans and low caste non-Aryans—the conqueror and the conquered.*

According to Irfan Habib (Caste and Money in Indian History, p-9), "the period from the rise of Buddhism (500 B.C.) to the Gupta age (4th and 5th centuries A.D.) may then, be supposed to be the period of the formation of the Indian Caste System".

As a rigid form of division of labour, the caste system formed part of the relation of production. In fact, the caste system helped to maintain not a fabric of purity but a system of class exploitation. The hereditory occupation fixed by caste was necessary to enable 'special skill' to be 'accumulated from generation. (Marx, Capital, I, PP 331). The caste system provided another advantage to the ruling class by giving low status to the artisans (weaver and shoe-makers are untouchables). *The low status for artisans helped to curtail their power of resistance, thereby keeping wage-costs low.*

The course of our history shows tribal elements being fused into a general society with village economy. So caste does not seem to arise out of any internal division of a particular tribe but arose for an external process altogether. The different tribes entered the 'general society' carrying with them their primitive endogamous customs into that society thereby endogamy became a part of the caste system. If the tribe was already an agricultural community, it turned into a peasant caste (Shudra) of that particular territory. The separation of the peasant and menial castes clearly represented a division of labour. From Jatakas, we learn that there had been "manufacturers" villages peopled by smiths and carpenters. Thus *different craftsmen seem to have developed into specific castes.* A similar process of differentiation, based on growth of commerce led to the creation of Vaishya Caste.

Originally, Brahmans were purely the sacrificial priest and his principal source of livelihood was the fee at the sacrifice. The sacrifices (yajna) being performed mainly for success in war, the priests gained a great deal from the constant warface of petty tribal chiefs or kings. Because there was no payment to the peasant for the sacrificial animals and robbers plundered traders; both Vaishyas and Shudras suffered.

The advance of agrarian village economy over tribal community is the first great social revolution: the change from an aggregate of gentes to society. The increasing density of village settlements inevitably brought about transformations of the superstructure. The warrior tribes transformed into oligarch over a conquered population and those without weapons could survive only as guilds. As a result both local and invading tribes were being absorbed into the society. The transition from tribe or guild to caste means primarily an enrolment of a group in a hierarchial scheme of society. *The kings could rise above tribal restrictions only when he became independent of tribal property i.e. after the emergence of village economy with the system of private property.* In fact, the kings used Brahmans and village settlement to make themselves independent of tribal usage and tribal economy and to introduce caste and the Brahmans accepted all sorts of local superstition, ritual, worship, even service of guilds. The adherence to village economy was secured by the caste system with minimum of force at the price of perpetuating primitive belief and observances of class exploitation.

4

Historical Development of Caste System

Caste, an organisation of social inequality was built on the base of the prevailing material condition of living and was modified according to economic changes. The four Varna division of ancient society of our country had been possible only when pastoral Aryans took to agriculture and overpowered the local pre-Aryans subjugating them as slaves.

When the Aryans came to India they seem to have divided into three social classes: Warriors, Priests and common people. In the nomadic stage, Aryans used to live chiefly on the produce of cattle. When they settled down and took to agriculture, there was development of handicrafts also particularly for production of agricultural tools. As a result, there arose many occupations such as carpentry, pottery, smithery etc. for the common people. The three social classes of Aryans were designated as Kshatriya, Brahman and Vaisya; they were distinguished by the adjective of 'dwija' i.e. twice born (first being physical birth and second the initiation into caste). Non-Aryans and those of mixed origin, were designated as Shudra's. According to Rigveda, the dispossessed and impoverished Aryans also were relegated to the status of 'Shudra's. *The formation of Shudra caste was possibly helped by the pre-existence of temple slaves at Harappa*, an institution for which there is some archeological support in the barrack-like quarters found. The aboriginal tribes were left out and some of them along with 'Shudra's who used to do unclean work, like scavanging and disposal of nightsoil formed the group of "Untouchable".

During the Rigvedic period, Aryans had little or no consciousness of caste. Professions were not hereditory and there was neither any rule limiting marriages nor taboos on whom one could eat with. In that society war was a legitimate source of livelihood and later on it became a legitimate function of the Kshatriyas. With development of agriculture and growing specialisation of labour, the warriors-*Kshatriyas* b*ecame all the more important because on them depended the proctection of private property*. Thus Kshatriyas emerged as the dominant power and had the first rank in Varna division. The priests (Brahmans) came next, followed by the traders and money lenders (Vaishyas) and finally the cultivators (Shudras) had the lowest rank. Thus producers of food and wealth having low social status, contempt for manual labour was institutionalised in the Varna or Caste System; the upper caste mental workers became alienated from lower caste manual workers.

Vedic king, a Kshatriya was primarily a military leader. The pre-Aryan 'dashyu's were defeated by the Aryan chief 'Trasadashyu', one of the different names for Indra. In the religious sphere his role was negligible but gradually there was a change in the position of the king due to emergence of the idea of divinity in kingship. Special sacrifices were evolved to bestow divinity on the king through priests. Coronation became a religious ceremony. Thus began interdependence of 'Kshatriya's and 'Brahman's (Military and Civil) the two classes of exploiters and oppressors of common people. 'Vaishya's joined them at a later date but became the exploiters in the economic sphere. Kingship not only became divine but also hereditory. The monarchial system lent heavily on religious orthodoxy. *Caste institution with religious sanction was accorded higher status than any political institution.* The function of the king was to protect and maintain social order and defending social order was held to be the sacred duty of the king. Loyalty to social order was actuated, mainly through caste institution. Duties assigned to defferent castes became "dharma". *In monarchies, tribal loyalty weakened and gave way to caste loyalty.*

During Vedic period, as a result of the use of wooden plough (without iron tip) and indiscriminate killing of cattle in sacrifices, there had been little surplus in agricultural production, whereas the use of iron ploughshare, rise of towns and large scale trade in post-Vedic society led to prosperity in the economic condition. Around nine hundred B.C., *the use of iron made clearing of forests a less arduous task and there had been remarkable development of agriculture.* With the clearing of forests, rivers became the natural highway of trade and numerous settements on river banks acted as markets. The landowners who could employ others to cultivate their land were the potential traders. Thus *merchants arose from landowners.*

Wood being a material basic to life, cutting rather than burning was the more usual form of land clearing. The carpenter, the maker of plough and chariot, built boats which were useful in trade. Increasing availability of wood from forests made carpentry a lucrative profession which gave it honourable status in the society. In Rigveda, carpenter has been referred to as 'tvasta' and Bhrigu Muni, the compiler of Manusamhita was originally a carpenter by profession. Other essential members of the village community were metal workers particularly the blacksmiths (who made axes and choppers), potters, tanners, and weavers.

In ancient India, as in other countries, a conflict had been going on between tribal organisation (republic) and monarchy (kingdom). The republics of tribes of Vedic age began to lose their essential democratic character; some republican tribes belonging to Kshatriya as well as Sudra castes. The decline of tribal culture, in combination with a growing dependence on agrarian economy stimulated growth of monarchies which became patrons of caste system. Kingship initially become hereditory with a preference for Kshatriya caste. However, this preference remained theoretical, since kings of all four Varnas are known to have ruled.

Buddhism had little or no effect on the caste system because in Buddhist literature there is little or no direct criticism of the system. Even though Buddhist scriptures worked out duties of man regardless of caste, wealth and profession, 'Dhammapada's last chapter is entitled as "Brahman Varga" specifying the qualities of Brahman but contained not a word about other varnas! However, *influenced by Buddhism, non-Brahmans, in general, began to assert themselves in their own profession; reverence for Brahmans subtantially diminished.*

It was during the Upanishadic period when the caste system was ideologically fortified through the doctrines of 'Karma' and 'Rebirth'. Voice against this utterly reactionary philosophy was raised by the materialist philosophers (Lokayatic) who are commonly known as 'Charvaka's. Both Buddhists and Jainas were believers in 'Karma' and 'Rebirth'; as a result despite their disapproval and opposition to the caste system, the theoretical foundation remained unaffected. However, when Buddhism enjoyed royal patronage and its edicts were preached in Pali instead of Sanskrit, the language of upper caste Aryans, the common people, non-Brahmans became attracted towards Buddhism. *Brahmans were isolated from the common people and Buddhist 'Sraman's became very popular.*

In *413 B.C. there had been a momentous even—the people of Magadha deposed the last king* of the dynasty of Bimbisara-

Ajatashatru and appointed Shishunaga as the king. He was succeeded by 'Nanda's who were of low caste-Shudra. Mahapadma Nanda, the founder was the son of a Shudra mother; some say that he was born of the union of a barber with courtesan. Since that time, most of the leading dynasties of northern India belonged to castes other than Kshatriyas. And there had been a *reversal of the roles of Brahmans and Kshatriyas.* The religious teachers were Kshatriyas and some of the kings were Brahmans. Pushyamitra was the first important Brahman King who as the army chief, assassinated Brihadratha, the last Mauryan King. *Since then, Brahmans had a sort of rejuvenation.*

Chandra-gupta, the founder of Mauryan empire belonged to the Vaisya caste; but his prime minister and guide was the Brahman—Kautilya, popularly known as 'Chanakya'. Chandragupta was converted to Jainism and his grandson Asoka to Buddhism. Thus, Brahmanism lost royal patronage during Mauryan rule. It was during the reign of Asoka, the clearing of forests and settlement of new areas was organised by the government. The Shudras under the state control were put to work as cultivator in new areas thereby making large scale slavery unnecessary for cultivation. Obviously it was not liberalism on the part of Indian ruling class not to introduce the European type of slavery.

In those days, what was immutable was not slavery or freedom but caste. Megasthanes wrote: "No one is allowed to marry outside his caste, or exercise any calling or art except his own". From his description, we learn that magistrates and councilors were Brahmans or Kshatriyas; and herdsmen either a Shudra or an outcaste. Salaries paid to different categories are very telling: the chief minister, the purohita and the commander of the army 48,000 panas, the treasurer and chief collector 24.000 panas; the accountants and clerks—500 panas and artisans—120 panas! During Asoka's rule, there had been conflict between the economically powerful Vaishyas (Shresthis) and the two upper castes; the Vaisyas became the chief patrons of Buddhism and Jainism.

The rise of mercantile community occurred during the period—200 B.C. to 300 A.D. and there had been a large number of foreigners in port twons and trade centres. They were gradually assimilated through their becoming a number of subcastes. However, conversion of an individual had always been a problem because of placing them into a caste which is hereditory i.e. dependant on birth. It was for Greeks, Kushans and Shakas to become fallen Kshatriyas or Buddhists. This opportunity was taken advantage of by some Shudra artesans who raised their status of caste by changing occupations. *The rising importance of Vaishyas and the creation of new subcastes must have caused concern to Brahmans*, the upholders of social laws and conduct, and social relationship between different groups of people had to be specified. *The result was the writing of Manu's Dharmashastra and other Smriti-Shastras.* Manu-Samhita compiled by Bhrigu clearly states that the *book is meant to establish supremacy of Brahmans over other castes.*

By seventh century B.C. tribal communities gave way to more stable republics and monarchies. Village lands were split into private holdings or owned by local rulers; *the communal ownership declined.* During Mauryan rule, the majority of population lived in villages. The clearing of land and settlement of new areas were organised by the state and a large number of Shudras were deported from overpopulated areas and employed to clear waste land. *Thus 'Shudra's were slaves under state control.* Slavery was a recognised institution at that time; *Megasthanes testified the existence of domestic slaves.* However, slavery in our country was probably not as much immutable as in Greek society. Caste slavery, of course, was immutable. 'Shudra's according to Manusamhita, can never be liberated.

Brahmanism helped the maintenance of caste-stratified social order in which 'Kshatriya's fought. 'Brahman's prayed, 'Vaishya's paid and 'Shudra's served. This arrangement worked well upto the stage when the mode of production was primitive and all power rested with the king. *It was during the reign of Bimbishara, the beginning of an administrative system took root.* Each village was under the jurisdiction of a headman who acted as the tax collector for royal treasury. With the king as the state authority. the kingdoms continued smoothly till the second half of the third century A,D.—the beginning of 'Kali' age, a period of natural calamity followed by an acute crisis in economic and social order. *The most significant change in the economy of the following period was the large scale transfers of land to both secular and religious elements by kings.* The process is attested by a large number of charters recorded on copper plates which mostly grant villages with fiscal and administrative immunity to priests, vassals and officials. *The process of land grants made royal authority ineffective even in small kingdoms.*

In the epics and Puranas, the period (*Kali age*) has been referred to as the state of affairs in which the common people were oppressed with taxes and forced labour. Mahabharata (III, 188, 71) reads: "nirvisesha janapada karavistibhirarditah" i.e. taxes (kara) affected the Vaishyas and forced labour (visti) the 'Shudra's. Artisans and peasants revolted; they not only refused to pay taxes but also refrained from performing the functions assigned to them according to their castes. Collection of taxes being impossible, royal treasury had no money to pay priests, administrators, army and numerous government officials. As an alternative, the practice for land-grant was adopted on a wide scale. *The State was relieved of the responsibility of maintaining law and order in the donated villages which became the sole concern of grant beneficiaries who were mostly Brahmans (priests) and* Kshatriyas (administrators). Shudras were provided with land as tenants or sharecroppers. From state slave status they were elevated to the status of peasant and permitted to participate in rituals. *Thus in villages a new production relation* emerged—*Vedic 'gopati's changed to Buddhist 'gahapat's and finally to 'Bhupati's as a result of royal land grant.*

With development of private ownership of land it became necessary to preserve carefully the family history of caste or lineage concerned. *Caste became hereditory: Varna to Jati.* The king as Bhumidar or giver of land delegated royal authority to the grant beneficiary and on this strength the latter claimed taxes from cultivators and artisans. The grant-beneficiaries became the defacto landowners and they ruled over the villages as the local agents of the king, the supreme authority of the Kingdom.

The importance of land-ownership is best expressed as: "Yashya yashya yada bhumih, tasya sada phalam". With land grants and practical status derived thereof, the Brahmans forged many charters (Kuta-sasana) and claimed enjoyment of villages on that basis. Most of those charters asked the peasants or 'Shudra's to carry out the orders of the beneficiaries. These orders related not only to payment of taxes, but also the general control over Shudra's labour power. This labour could be used either in the fields cultivated by the peasant or in those directly managed by the beneficiary. Thus the beneficiary of the land grant achieved blanket authority over the Shudra peasant through various charters and extracted obedience without protest.

In addition to Brahmans and administrators, land grant beneficiaries included monastary and temple. As a result, *political and economic control became vested with religious institntions.* Buddhist monastarics in eastern India, temples in south India and many priests in upper and middle Gangetic plains, central India, Deccan and Assam became the principal religious beneficiaries. Non-religious such as tribal chiefs in Orissa, were elevated to the position of landowner. Generally speaking, landowners almost all of whom belong to upper castes became the ruling class of the society, and common people in the villages were subjected to social and economic exploitation. The unequal distribution of land and powcr caused by the land grant created new social groups and ranks which did not fit in with the fourfold varna system, *There occurred a proliferation of castes and subcastes.*

In South India. tenancy was of two kinds: land held in communal ownership or privately held by individual peasant who paid the tax to royal tax collector or the temple which acted as the tax collector, banker and money lender. Unlike the northern Indian Brahman land-owners, the southern counter-parts were more adventurous and invested their surplus income in commerce. *Brahmans in certain areas became trading caste.* Thus Brahmans of South India, economically more prosperous through landownership and trade became virtually the masters and the Shudras the slaves working for them.

Brahmans naturally stressed upon caste loyalties and caste assemblies so that wider basic unity among the non-Brahmans did not develop. Communal differences were already proving very convenient for the upper caste.

Caste status was modified by the economic status. For example, administrators of the court were non-Brahmans but they were given special privileges. Those who engraved the copper plate charters, weavers who woved the dress of royal family or stone masons working in temples or palaces were exempt from certain dues and even when they were of low castes, they were regarded with greater respect than other members of their own castes.

The relationship of caste with occupation did not always adhere strictly to the rules of legal and social codes. During Gupta age, political pressure on Shudras was lessened but economic exploitation and social oppression became more direct and severe.

During the medieval period artisans and merchants were given feudal titles indicating military and administrative ranks. According to inscriptions of "Bengal" (III, 5, 36), head of the artsans of Varendra, held the title of 'ranaka'. Certain titles such a. Thakur, Raut, Nayaka etc. were confined to not only the Kshatriyas or Rajputs but were also conferred on Kayasthas and members of other castes who were granted land and who served in the army. The constant transfer of land or land revenue led in early medieval times to the emergence of a scribe known as 'Kayastha.'

A large number of writers and record keepers had to be employed to maintain records of the lands and villages and of revenue which were given in grants. Since Gupta period, the beginning of fragmentation of land on account of the laws of the partition of landed property made the maintenance of the details of the individual plots necessary. Village and land records had to be carefully recorded in order to avoid and settle land disputes which were very common. The whole work was done by a class of writers, who were known by different names such as Kayastha, Karana, Karanika etc. Like Brahmans who formed only one class of priests out of seventeen kinds of priests in Vedic times, Kayasthas formed only one class of a dozen kinds of writers or record keepers.

The Brahmans were faced with the problem of finding a place for the Kayasthas in the Varna system: the lawgivers connected them with both the Shudras as well as the dvijas. Calcutta High Court called them the Shudras whereas the Allahabad High Court called them Brahmans. Kalhan, however, noted that Brahman-Sivaratha was appointed as a Kayastha official. The rise of the Kayasthas as a professional literate caste undermined, to an extent, the monopoly of Brahmans as writers and scribes. Kayasthas serving as Ministers were held in higher status than Brahmans and this was resented by the latter. The Brahmans were also angry with the Kayasthas because they maintain records of land grants with which the former were mainly concerned. As a result, *the Kayasthas never appeared in favourable light in Brahmanical literature.* The lawgiver-Yajnavalkya mentioned about *Kayasthas* (as early as the fourth century A.D.) *as oppressor of subjects.*

The Varna system was modified by the rise of landowning class connected with the administration of villages and also by the change in the relative position of Vaishyas and Shudras. In post-Gupta times, the Shudras no longer appear only as slaves, artisans and agricultural labourers. They take the place of Vaishyas as cultivators. Al-Biruni noted the absence any significant difierence between Vaishyas and Shudras. From the beginning of the Christian era, 'Smriti's approximated the Vaishyas to the position of Shudras. By sixth century A.D. the Vaishyas became traders and merchants; no longer they remained peasant cultivator. As traders, the Vaishyas had been well. But in post-Gupta period there was decline in trade and they suffered in social rank. Brahmanism advanced in Bengal and South India in Gupta and post-Gupta times. The advent of Rajputs had thrown the original Kshatriya varna into background.

Hinduism spread over distant parts of the country but the fourfold Varna system did not diffuse uniformly in all areas. For example, in Northern India, there had been a large number of castes grouped under Kshatriya and Vaishya varnas whereas in Bengal and South India there were practically no Kshatriyas or Vaishyas. The progress of Brahmanism was not in the form of mass migration; the tribal population in the peripheral regions were admitted to the Brahmanial systems mainly as Shudras who might have been conquered by the Kshtriyas or Rajputs but their acculturation was carried by the Brahmans.

The early medieval period was the period when there had been proliferation and fragmentation in the varna system. The existing varnas were split up into many castes and numerous new tribes were annexed to and incorporated within them. The process of proliferation appears to be most striking among the Brahmans. Many Brahman castes were named after the ritual they practised or the branch of Vedic learning they cultivated. In land charters the Brahmans are identified by their 'Gotra' (ancestry-male), by the branch of Vedic learning and the village to which they belonged. In course of time, they came to the be recognised only by their Gotra and family traditions. In Deccan and South India, it is difficult to be certain about the purity and continuity of the Gotra and family traditions, because members of non-Aryan tribes seem to have been given the Aryan Gotras. In land charters, the original homes of Brahmans are mentioned and since Gupta period, a Brahman is recognised by the village to which he belonged.

In the Kshatriya community, proliferation was caused by the emergence of Rajputs. The practice of ascribing solar and lunar origins to ruling dynasties in inscriptions began from about 7th century. It was in medieval times, the rule of 'Kshatriya Raja Uchyate' became operative. The Bactrian Greeks, Sakas, Parthians were absorbed as second class Kshatriyas. Since the 5th and 6th centuries A.D. Kshatriya castes multiplied; Hunas and Gurjars joined the rank of Kshatriya as Rajputs. Solankis (Chalukyas), Paramas, Chahamanas, Tomars etc. had central Asian origin. It is not true that all foreigners were aceepted as Kshatriyas. Gurjars broke into Brahmans, Vanias, Potters, Goldsmiths who are looked upon as Shudras (Dr. Bhandarkar).

In Bengal and South India, there had been no foreign invasion. So there only the ruling chiefs of local tribes were admitted as Kshatriyas, and the vast majority of their kinsman were condemned to the position of Shudras.

The Shudras had the largest number of castes and sub-castes. The earliest law-books mention only about a dozen of castes of mixed origin but Manu-Samhita enumerates *61 mixed castes*. (MS, 1-51). Additional Shudra castes mentioned in Brahmavaivarta Purana added to Manu's list would make it 100. Vishnudharmottara Purana mentions that thousands of mixed castes are produced as a result of the connection of Vaishya women with men of lower castes. The conquest of aboriginal people living in the jungles added to the number and variety of Shudra castes. The conquest of the backward peoples living in forests and hilly regions by Brahmanised kings from agriculturally advanced areas enormously added to the number and variety of Shudra castes. The suppression of Sabaras, Bhils, Pulindas etc. is referred to in medieval inscriptions from Central India. According to Bhagavan Singh Suryavamsi, Deccan powers fought against the Abhiras for five hundred years but the latter could not be assimilated into Brahmanical order.

The middle ages saw a phenomental increase in the number of impure Shudras or Untouchables, who were first noted in the fourth century B.C. by Panini. Untouchables are referred to in madieval texts as those eating cow and they were listed as Antyajas, Barata, Baruda, Bheda, Bhilla, Candala, Dasa, Neta, Rajaka. Most of the Untouchables were backward tribes. Twelve categories of Untouchables are mentioned in early medieval lawbooks, but the actual number is much more. Most Untouchables were inducted into the Hindu system through the spread of Hinduised Buddhism.

Transformation of crafts into castes had been responsible for the multiplication of Shudra castes. Napita, Modaka, Tambulika, Svarnakara, Malakara, Sankhakara, Sutrakara, Citrakara etc. are all called mixed castes, in medieval texts (Brahmavaivarta Purana) emerging out of various crafts.

Religious affiliation also led to proliferation of castes. Members of different sections began to behave as members of a caste. The Lingayats and Virasaivas in Karnataka and Radhaswamis in Northern India formed separate castes. In the Gangetic Valley, the goalas who worshipped Krishna and regarded themselves to be racially related to him called themselves 'Kisnots'.

The original varna system was modified by the following facts:

1. Transformation of Shudras into cultivators
2. Relegation of Vaishyas to the position of Shudras
3. Transformation of Vaishyas (vis-common people) to merchants
4. Land grants to religious and non-religious individuals and institutions
5. Buddhism, Jainism and Bhakti (devotional) cult which inculcated abject surrender to the authority.

It is recognised by all that the background to social changes is always provided by certain economic developments. Castes or varnas were originally related to the labour of production. According to Manu, there are seven approved ways of acquiring wealth; legacy, gain, purchase, conquest, agriculture, trade and acceptance of gifts. The first three of these were permissible for all castes, the fourth exclusively for Kshatriya and the last for Brahman (M.S.X. 116-7). *Brahmans and Kshatriyas must not engage themselves in 'vriddhi' i.e. in activities of production.* So, agriculture, arts and crafts became the call of the lower castes and the task of administration that of upper castes. This division into two categories of mental and manual workers was possible when a section of the community could live on the surplus produced by another section. The producers were manual workers. The leissured class who withdrew from the responsibility of direct manual labour also withdrew from the obligation of acknowledging the reality of material world and this resulted in philosophical enquiry taking free flight into the realm of knowledge divorced from action. *Thus grew the idealist philosophy giving primacy to spirit or mind over matter or reality. Caste is a product of idealist philosophy.*

In Gupta period (A.D. 300-700) generally described by the religious Hindus as the 'classical' age, the upper caste Hindus had a good living standard. The Gupta Kings had been the patrons of the caste system. However, this situation was restricted to Madhyadesh only. The 'Kama-Sutra' of Vatsayan was written during this period and the life style of the upper castes during the period was aptly described. 'Geeta' was probably composed at that time and incorporated in the 'Mahabharata' eulogiring the role of Krishna as the creator of 'Chaturvarnya'. Krishna was probably a Shudra, at least by being brought up as a child of that caste. It is during this period, Shudras were allowed to read a Shastra-Mahabharata. However, the relationship between caste and occupation was maintained. The status of Shudras improved as compared to Mauryan times. In the legal literature, a clear distinction was made between Shudra and slave. The emphasis on Brahman purity was increased and correspondingly increased stress was laid on the impurity of outcastes. Fa-hsien has mentioned about the fear of pollution. During Gupta period were written the Puranas, popular memories were rewritten in a prophetic form and they became the Brahmanical inter-pretations of the past.

During the 6th and 7th centuries, A.D. in South India, Tamil devotionalism achieved a great deal of popularity. The Brahmans were obsessed with caste regulations and rigidly excluded non-Brahmans from participation in religious knowledge. In the beginning, Brahmans did not support Tamil devotional cult since Saiva saints not only ignored caste but accepted even non-Hindus. Later on, when Saivites accepted Brahman supremacy, there was a compromise. It was in South India including Rajasthan that the Brahmans did not permit Shudras and Untouchables to enter the precints of the temples.

During the period of 900-1200 A.D. South India was ascendant in the Indian scene and caste consciousness had become a marked feature in social relationship. In the South, there is little importance of the two castes of Kshatriya and Vaisya; the two principal castes were Brahman and Shudra. Shudras are divided there into clean and urclean. During this period, temples became the centre of social and economic life, particularly in rural areas. Caste-consciousness became prominent in rural areas. Caste consciousness became so prominent that Brahmans confident of their dominant position enjoying special privileges stood out distinct from the rest of the society. *They owned land and enjoyed royal support.* Unlike north Indian Brahman land-owners, the southern Brahmans were more adventurous and invested surplus income in commerce. The Brahmans were in control of powerful positions; in effect they became the virtual ruler of the Hindu society. Ramanuja, the great religious leader of the South though a supporter of privileges for Brahmans was opposed to the excluding of Shudras from worship of Gods in the temple. But his pleadings had no effect.

'Rajatarangini' by Kalhan (written between 1148 and 1150 A.D.) pointed out that in Kashmir, Brahmans were Kayasthas. It appears that the office of Kayastha was open to all people irrespective of caste; even a gardener could become a Kayastha. Obuiously, Kayastha was not the name of the any caste. About Kayasthas, he wrote "For, indeed, the officials like cholera, colic and wagering snakes smite the world swiftly and are another epidemic for the subjects. The crab kills his father, the white ant destroys its mother, but the ungrateful functionary, when he has obtained office destroys every body. . the bureaucrat and the poison tree, it is amazing, render the very ground on which they prosper, difficult to access". As for Candalas, both Kalhan and Al-Biruni said that *they were used as hired assassins. In Kalhan's time, untouchability was unknown in Kashmir.* Low castes mentioned by him are Nishads, Kirats, Kaivartas, Dombas. Svapach and Candalas. According to Kalhan, *cast considerations did not matter in the selection of the royal spouse.* King Chakravarman married an 'Untouchable' Domba woman. But Dombas were not exactly untouchable, as known in other parts of India. The point to note is that intermediate castes between Brahmans and lower castes were unknown in other parts of

India. The point to note is that intermediate castes between Brahmans and lower castes were unknown in Kashmir.

Rajputs enter the scene of Indian history during the 11th century. They were of foreign origin and the Brahmans gave them royal lineage and accorded the status of Kshatriya in the caste system. Most authorites accept the view that they were either descended from the Huns or from those tribes who had entered India along with Hun invaders. The four clans which claimed Agnicula origin dominated early Rajput activities.

In the 11th century, Rajendra Chola extended his kingdom as far north as the Ganges and from the north-west began Muslim raids headed by Mahammud of Ghazni. *By 12th century, feudalism was well established, the aristocracy consisted of feudatories including Brahmans.* Grants to Brahmans were meant to acquire religious merit; they performed sacrifices for the king who patronised the Brahmans who, in turn, showed their gratitude and composed famous genealogies for the king. During this period, Manu-Samhita was accorded high authority and *Dayabhaga and Mitakshara became the basis of civil law.* The prosperity of money-lenders increased and caste consideration in the matter of money-lending was regularised. The Brahmans were charged two per cent whereas the Shudras five per cent or more interest on the same capital loan. The caste structure was made more water-tight. In the contest of supremacy between Brahmans and Vaishyas, the former having acquired political power by becoming landowners emerged as the victors. The desire for exclusiveness on the part of Brahmans led to an obsession with keeping aloof from lower castes and untouchability regulations became stricter. *Untouchability was extended to even higher caste people who were opposed to Brahmanism.* The two intermediate castes—Kshatriya and Vaishya did not conform fully to caste regulations and a number of subcastes emerged from intermarriage between these two castes. Amongst the subcastes, the most important was 'Kayastha'—the clerks of administratlon who wrote documents and maintained administration records. Some of these Kayasthas received land grants and became landlords. Certain subcastes began to claim origin fıom higher castes; for example, the Khatris claimed that they are of Kshatriya origin but they took to commerce thereby receiving the status of a Vaisya. The Gujars, Jats and Ahirs all claimed Kshatriya origin.

The period of mercantile activity and the movement of population from one region to another had accelerated the formation of subcastes. Foreigners refer to seven instead of four principal castes. These seven castes consist of four basic castes and three sub-castes. Al Idrisi (12th century) wrote about 7 castes; nobility, Brahmans, soldiers, cultivators, artisans, singers and entertainers, Obviously by caste he meant occupational ranks only.

The beginning of thirteenth century marks a 'break' in Indian history. It was caused not only by the intrusion of Islam but also the emergence of 'Oriental Despotism'. The caste structure continued to be essentially the same as in the earlier period; the attitude of the Muslims towards the caste system was by no means one of disapprobation. Muslims censured polytheism and idol worship of Hindusim and never bothered about the social inequity of caste system. Al-Beruni (C. 1030) was the only exception; as a scientist he said: "We Muslims, of course stand entirely on the other wide of the question, considering all men are equal, except in piety". (India, I, p. 100). However, the historian Barani (Tarikh-i-Feroz-Shahi) clamoured for a hierachial order based on birth. *Muslim regimes protected the Hindu caste system because it helped to generate a larger revenues from the villages and lower the wage-costs of artisans in cities.*

The caste system, however, had to undergo certain adjustments as a result of the new circumstances. The new ruling classes and their dependents brought not only demand for new products and new kinds of services but also fairly wide range of new craft technology, such as rightangled gearing for Persian wheel, the spinning wheel, paper manufacture, vault construction, use of bitumen and lime cement and iron horse-shoe. Thus it was necessary to create new professions and to learn new devices. As a result there had been a considerable expansion of artisan population. *The pressure of the new circumstances led to a large scale slave-trading and the emergence of slave labour as a significant component of urban labour.* The number of slaves in the Sultan's establishments were very high (50,000 under Alauddin Khilji, and 1,80,000 under Feroz Tughlug). *Slaves were deprived of caste and converted to Islam*; they could be put to any tasks or learn any trade. They probably created, along with artisan immigrants, the core of Muslim labouring community.

Conversion of free Hindu elements, some of whom splitting off from their parent bodies in search of higher social status or willing to take to occupations or practices not permitted to them previously, also took place, thereby creating a substantial Muslim population in India. On these converted communities there was definite influence of the caste system. For example, the Muslim weavers, butchers and barbars had strong tendencies to be endogamous. The 'Kalmin' communities among Muslims, though not untouchables like Hindu outcastes, were held in contempt. Nonetheless, Muslim population, in general, remained outside the caste framework.

The mono-theistic beliefs of Islam and the legal equality of Muslim community exercised certain influence on Hindu caste system. Monotheistic movements stressed on equality and condemned caste and ritual observances and most of the preachers belonged to low castes; *Namdev*, a calico-printer, *Kabir*, a weaver, *Raidas*, a scavenger, *Sain* a barber, *Dadu*, a cotton carder and *Dhanna*, a jat peasant.

By the 16th century, a pattern of living had evolved in which a considerable degree of assimilation had taken place. But among the upper strata, certain resentments remained. The very fact that the Indian Muslims were mostly converts from low Hindu castes irritated the upper caste Hindus and *in the process of preserving their exclusiveness and retaining the social privileges the Brahmans concentrated upon their own resources and tradition. This led to a sort of revivalism of the past.* This tendency affected the anti-British nationalist movement led by Indian National Congress.

During 15th and 16th centuries, a number of 'Bhakti saints appeared on the scene e.g. Kabir, Nanak, Sri Chaitanya. Both Kabir and Nanak thought that caste and religion were keeping Indian people apart. Their stress was on a re-ordering of the society free from caste and religious restrictions. Both of them firmly denunciated caste but *Kabir-panthis were rejected by Muslims in general.* Nanak succeeded in forming a new sect which however did not escape caste influence.

During 19th century, Rammohan Roy edited and published the Sanskrit work "Vajrasuchi", a treatise directed against the institution of caste. 'Atmasakti' founded by him (in 1815) carried on agitation against the caste system. However, he was famous for his opposition to 'Sati' custom, not for crusade against caste. It is interesting to note that despite his antipathy towards the caste system, he continued to wear the 'sacred' thread' of Brahmans. Bankim Chandra Chattopadhyaya and Ramendra Sunder Trivedi strongly criticised the caste system and the role of Brahmans. Ironically, M.K. Gandhi who had been very vocal in his sympathy for the 'untouchables' *never uttered a word, even indirectly criticising the caste system.* About his stand on the question of caste, the less said the better.

During the second half of the nineteenth century, toiling masses from rural areas began to crowd into old towns and the newer trading and administrative centres and as long-distance trade grew, the general monetization of the economy developed further; pressure upon the land inereased and Western education penetrated deeper. In Bihar, over a period of centuries, Rajputs, Bhumihars (cultivating Brahmans) and Brahmans had established a clear dominance in economic and political power. *The economic dominance of Rajputs, Brahmans and Bhumihars was reinforced by their numerical strength.* They formed the landowning class. The 'raiyats' or peasants are all of low castes .As fixed by 1873 Act, the revenue demand of ninetenths of the rent was exacting and the landowners extracted in addition to the rent abwabs and salaami—illegal cesses from the peasant tenants. The Maharajah of Dumrao also extorted illegal cesses like ghee, curds and fuel at the time of funerals, marriages or festivals in the family. The peasants had to pay. The backward caste peasants became agitated with the apprehesion that the upper castes who were being organised with the tacit connivance of British imperialists would increase their tyranny, In Bihar, the major backward castes are Ahirs, Kurmis and Keoris who together constitute about a third of the total population. The Ahir movement developed around 1914 in Patna District; the Gopi Jatiya Sabha that was formed in 1912 spread to all cow-herding castes of all over North India from Punjab to Bengal. Kurmis also joined the organisation. In 1934, the Triveni Sangh symbolised a united organisation of Ahirs, Kurmis and Keoris. The Sangh had a membership of 1,000,000. The Indian National Congress organised other sections of the lower castes in the Depressed Classes League under Jagjivan Ram. However, Untouchables and Muslims became members of the Triveni Sangh. Ultimately in 1946, Triveni Sangh members contested the election on Congress ticket. In 1948, the Sangh merged with INC-sponosored Backward Classes Federation. Consequently, the backward caste movement failed to develop. It is ironic that the Sangh leaders who sought guidance from Swami Sahajanand Saraswati, the Bhumihar messiah did not have the necessary leadership from him.

The ceilings Act resulted in large scale resumption of leased land and consequent ejection of tenant peasants. The sharecropper had to bear the brunt of bad harvets. He, however, could count on his 'banihars' a labourer who is provided with a certain amount of land (Kola) for attached labour. The banihars are mostly Chamars and Mushahars who live like animals in hovels, subsisting on master's 'Kesari'—a feed made of husk. *For them, wearing a clean dhoti, remaining seated in the presence of the master and even walking erect are taboo*!

A fundamental change in agrarian structure occurred in the mid 1970s as a result of abolition of absentee landlord system. Very large landowners had to sell land area above a certain ceiling to their tenants. There emerged a middle land-holding peasantry from the former tenant—cultivating section which comprised about 10% of the rural population. These middle peasants belonging to backward castes imitate their predecessor forward caste zamindar, in their attitude towards the landless agricultural labourers who are either Untouchables or of their own castes! Like the upper caste zamindars, they are also interested in perpetuating caste hierarchy!

The beginnings of the caste system

"The coming of the Aryans into India raised new problems —racial and political. The conquerd race, the Dravidians, had a long background of civilisation behind them, but there is little doubt that the Aryans considered themselves vastly superior and a wide gulf separated the two races. Then there was also the backward original tribes, nomads or forest dwellers. Out of this conflict and interaction of races gradually arose the caste system, which, in the course of succeeding centuries, was to affect Indian life so profoundly. Probably caste system was neither Aryan nor Dravidian. It was an attempt at social organisation of different races, a rationalisation of the facts as they existed at the time. It brought degradation in its train afterwards and *it is still a burden and a curse*; but we can hardly judge it from subsequent standards or later developments. It was in keeping with the spirit of the times and some such grading took place in most of the ancient civilisations, though apparently China was free from it. There was fourfold division in that other branch of the Aryans, the Iranians, during the Sassaman period, but it did not petrify into caste. Many of these old civilisations including that of Greece, were entirely dependent on mass slavery. There was no such mass or large scale labour slavery in India, although therc were relatively small number of domestic slaves. Plato in his Republic refers to a division similar to that of the four principal castes. Mediaeval catholicism knew this division also.

Caste began with a hard and fast division between Aryans and non-Aryans, the latter again being divided into the Dravidian races and the aboriginal tribes. The Aryans, to begin with, formed one class and there was hardly any specialisation. The word 'Arya' comes from a root word meaning to till, and the Aryans as a whole were agriculturists, and agriculture was considered a noble occupation. The tiller of the soil functioned also as priest, soldier, or trader, and there was no privileged order of priests. The caste divisions, originally intended to separate the Aryans from the non-Aryans, reacted on the Aryans themselves and as division of functions and specialisation increased, the new classes took the form of castes.

Thus at a time when it was customary for the conquerors to exterminate or enslave the conquered races, caste enabled a more peaceful solution which fitted in with the growing specialisation of functions. Life was graded and out of the mass of agriculturists evolved the Vaisyas, the agriculturists, artisans and merchants, the Kshatriyas, or rulers and warriors; and the Brahmins, priests and thinkers who were supposed to guide policy and preserve and maintain the ideals of the nation. Below these three there were the Shudras or labourers and unskiiled workers, other than the agriculturists. Among the indigenous tribes many were gradually assimilated and given a place at the bottom of the social scale, that is, among the

Shudras. This process of assimilation was a continuous one. These castes must have been in a fluid condition; rigidity came much later. Probably the ruling class had always great latitude, and person who by conquest or otherwise assumed power, could, if he so willed, joined the hierarchy as the Kshatriya, and get the priests to manufacture an appropriate genealogy connecting him with some ancient hero. The word Arya ceased to have any racial significance and came to mean noble, just as un-Arya means ignoble and was usually applied to nomadic tribes, forest dwellers etc."

Jawaharlal Nehru

5

Caste and Class

Caste has been defined in the "Encyclopaedia of Social Sciences" (Vol. 3, 1930 254b, 254b-7a) by Kroeber as follows: "Castes, therefore, are a special form of social classes, which in tendency at least are present in every society. Castes differ from social classes, however, in that customs and law attempt their rigid and permanent separation from one another. *Social classes are generic soil from which caste systems have at various times and places independently grown up*". In regard to the definition of caste, G.S, Ghurye's position is quite close to that of Kroeber. Hindu caste system is popularly understood as the division of the society into a five-fold hierarchy with Brahmans at the head, followed in order by Kshatriyas, Vaishyas, Shudras and lastly, the Untouchables. Caste in the above sense is referred to as 'Varna'. However, the real unit of caste system is not one of the five varnas but jati. There are innumerable jatis; Prof. Ghurye calculates that *there are about 2000 subcastes (jatis) in each linguistic area.*

Louis Dumont ('Social Inequality' p. 337) argues that there is a basic difference between Negro-White relation in America and the traditional caste in India; the former exists within a framework of equalitarian values while the latter accepts the values of inequality. It is very true that Hindu caste system is based on the recognition of inequality as a fundamental value. Moreover, the status group becomes a caste when its separation is secured not only through customs but principally ritual regulation (impurity through contact). He holds that caste is an expression of hierarchy—a consciously organised principle. *Thus caste is nothiug but a deliberate design meant to perpetuate social inequality* while class is a consequence of the development of productive forces resulting in social division of labour. According to Max Waber (Thc Religion of India), castes should be viewed as status groups and as such should be distinguished from *classes which are economic groups.* Castes play an important part in agricultural society and Michael Young (The Rise of Meritocracy, p. 24) has remarked "*The soil grows castes; the machine makes classes*", However. *classes did appear earlier than modern machines.*

The concept of class has close association with Marxism. The Marxist theory of class structure establishes first of all the existence of two mutually antagonistic groups engaged in the process of production. These are what one calls the 'basic classes'. They are distinguished from each other by their relations to production. One of these classes owns the means of production, the other is deprived of these although it is the one which operates them. This relationship determines the nature of the first as the exploiting class and of the second as the exploited class. For this reason, to many, the term 'class' has become a synonym for social inequality.

Social classes are de facto groups; one belongs to a class without doing anything specific to join it. Similarly one belongs to a caste by being born of parents of that particular caste. In case of caste, one has no option to discard it. Class groupings are open; one can enter or leave them with facility when one has the means to do so. Caste denotes a closed group characterised by the occupation of its members and the impossibility of entering or leaving it. However, there had been exceptions. Shivaji, a 'Maratha' by caste was accomodated as a 'Kshatriya'!

In regard to the origin of classes in society, Engels wrote: "Out of the first great social division of labour arose the first great division of the society into two classes-masters and slaves, exploiters and exploited" Christopher Caudwell (Studies and Further Studles in a dying Culture) pointed out: "Since classes are not arbitrary absolute creations, but come into being as specific developments of economy, *they are by no means inevitable*". *Classes arose spontaneously in societies when the primitive communal system was disintegrating and the slave system was emerging*; the development of private property in place of communal property increased the people's economic inequality. Some man, mainly the clan-chief became rich and seized the communal means of production; others deprived of the means of production were compelled to work for those who became their owners. So there emerged two principal classes-exploiter and exploited. Thus *class denotes economic relationship whereas caste indicates one's profession, social origin and the social status*.

According to Romila Thapar (From Lineage to State). "Theoretical construct of caste society was not the simple unfolding of class society, nor the mechanical measurement of ritual status. It was an attempt at interlocking series of social unity based on diverse rules of functioning but all in the context of lineage system. The initial attempt therefore, in the varna system was not to reflect a class system. In 'History of India' Vol. I. she also writes: "The actual mechanism of caste was not a formal division of society into four broad groups. The first three castes were probably a theoretical framework evolved by the Brahmans, into which they systematically arranged various professions. The fourth caste, however, appears to have been based on both race as well as occupation". Iravati Karve—(Cultural Heritage of India, Vol. II): "*Caste seems to be the device through which all racial and cultural elements were kept separate and intact in a small region, without complete extinction of even of the oldest and most primitive element . . Caste divides the whole Indian population into mutually exclusive, competitive, rival and jealous communities*".

From Avesta, we know of four classes in Iranian society. They are: (1) Athrob (priest) (2) Rothesta (warrior) (3) Vastro fashna (peasants) and (4) Huiti (artisans).

In Greece, there had been three classes: (1) Basilens (King), (2) Thet (independent citizen) (3) Doulos (slave).

In Rome, the three classes were: (1) Flamines (priest) (2) Milites (warrior) and (3) Quirits (common people).

In France, amongst kelts, there were three classes:

(1) Druides (priest) (2) Equites (warrior) (3) Plebes (common man).

In Anglosaxon England, the class division was:

(1) Erol, Earl (warrior or aristocrat) (2) Carol, Churl (free man).

It appears the social classes of priests, warriors and common people were common to many countries. The magicians turned to priests who were dependent on the ruling chief for their livelihood and they became the king-makers and spiritual leaders of society.

D.D. Kosambi (Culture and Civilization in Ancient India in Historical Outline) writes: "Caste is a class on a primitive level of production. . Theoretic system of varna is roughly that of classes whereas the observed castes and subcastes derive clearly from tribal groups of different ethnic origin . . The basic nature of caste need hardly be doubted, though it was still class on a primitive level of production". The noted historian R.K. Mukherji writes: (Glimpses of Ancient India) "Classes hardened into castes under the influence of heredity".

Classes arose as a result of usurpation of communal means of production whereas castes arose as a device to repress the physical workers. Caste was the creation of Brahmans or the idealist philosophers of ancient India. Plato (Laws): "We have now made excellent arrangements to free our citizens from the necessity of manual work: the business of arts and crafts has been passed on to others; agriculture has been handed over to slaves on condition of granting us a sufficient return to live in a fit and seemly fashion, how now shall we organise our lives? A still more pertinent question would have been—How will our new way of life reorganise our thoughts?" Thus was born in Greece the idealist philosophy which justified slavery and the society was divided into two groups: mental and manual workers. In India, the idealist philosophy of 'Karma' and 'rebirth' was harnessed to justify the caste system which also engendered contempt for manual labour.

Caste is commonly regarded as an extreme case of class. In fact, *Social classes are the generic soil from which caste system have grown up.* Castes differ from social classes in that they have emerged into social consciousness to the point that custom and law attest their rigid and permanent separation from one another. Caste is at once rigid whereas class is more flexible, vaguer and more widespread. Caste, at least theoretically, has nothing to do with production relation whereas class is fundamentally a manifestation of production relation. *Caste is a super-structure on the base of a class-divided society.* In emphasising the importance of caste in India, an author claiming to be Marxist goes to the extent of declaring that caste is a pre-class institution!! The taboo of untouchability is pre-class but caste division certainly not. Dr. Ambedkar rightly said that the caste system was an imposition by the ruling classes over the service classes. In sum, when property or means of production was no longer communal, on the base of class the superstructure of caste was built. *Introduction of caste system was a deliberate action on the part of the exploiting class.*

With regard to caste, almost every statement of a general nature may be contradicted. For example, the Brahmans are not to eat meat or any food derived from the taking of life. But it is well known that Vedic Brahmans ate beef, Kashmiri Brahmans eat meat, those in Bengal fish, without losing the caste. Caste is supposed to exist only for the Hindus and it may cut across the religious barrier. Roman Catholics in Goa who regard themselves as Brahman, will prefer to take food from a Hindu Brahman, but not from a "Shudra Christian"! This is so because Brahman Christians and Hindu Brahmans are both members of the land-owning class. Thus class interest respects caste discrimination.

Caste division can not always be identified with class division. There had been kings who belonged to castes other than Kshatriya, which should be the ruling caste. In practice. any ruler or an invader who extended his patronage to the Brahmans and gave at least nominal adherence to the tenets of some kind of Hinduism was given the honour of Kshatriya, even though his poor relations in some distant village may be treated as "Shudras".

The Brahmans, the king-pin of the caste system, originally were purely the sacrificial priest, the fee at the sacrifice being their main source of livelihood. The principal purpose of sacrifice was propitiation of gods and naturally sacrificial ceremonies were intended for success in war and the priests-Brahmans gained a great deal from the constant warfare. Buddhist 'Ahimsa' was directed not against meat-eating as such but against, the costly sacrifices by kings.

6

Political and Social Consequences of Caste System

The importance of caste in our country can not be over-emphasised. The first Backward Classes Commission admitted in its report: "It can not be denied that *caste system is the greatest hindrance in the way of our progress towards egalitarian society*".

Caste is not a mere custom or a measure of social status. It is the system of life for a Hindu. It penetrates every aspect of living in Hindu society. Ronald Segal (Crisis of India) gives an excellent description of caste: "Caste conditions how and when, and what and where a person eats, washes and talks and prays; from whom specific food and drinks and specific utensils may be taken, or to whom offered; the way the hair is worn, the kind of clothes, the shape of ornaments, the form of funeral, the frequency of sex (orthodox Brahmans in Tanjore make love only on Fridays)".

The traditional social system in our country was organised around caste structures and caste identities. In the past, our village had a distinctive design which reflected closely the basic values of Indian eivilization. During the medieval phase, many changes were introduced into the society but this did not affect the basic design of caste stratification of the society. Muslim rule brought in a few new crafts and some new elements were introduced into the population through settlement, conversion or both but it did not produce any new design to replace the old one. The new groups whether they practiced new craft or professed a new religion, were fitted into the existing social arrangements without altering the basic character. The changes were organisational rather than structural. The 19th century saw the emergence of forces which were contradictory to those which ensured the continuity of the basic design. This was not a question of supply of a new type of land revenue administration. What was at issue was something more fundamental, the basic value by which economic life in the village had been governed by the past—*the 'Jajmani, system was no longer tenable.*

N.K. Bose (The Structure of Hindu Society) spoke of two polar types of villages—the 'Tribal' and the 'Brahmanical'. The latter type is characterised by hierarchial caste stratification. According to him, Brahmanical type had three characteristics. (1) system of multiple gradation associated with an elaborate system of labour (2) vertical ties of diffuse and enduring nature between families and individuals and (3) hierarchial values among different members of the village. The gradations in the village may be seen most easily in term of its arrangement of castes and subcastes. A village generally has between 30 and 40 castes and subcastes. Social life is based primarily on an economy of land and grain. The village also made provisions for a variety of crafts and services. It is in the relations between agriculture, crafts and services that we see most clearly the distinctive design of the Indian village. When these relations undergo change, the design itself becomes eroded.

Participation in agriculture is elaborately graded. While scriptures and local customs allowed both Brahmans and scavengers to make a living from agriculture, their roles in the productive system are very different. Some lived off the rent from their land, others supervised work on their farms, yet others did various kinds of manual work either on their own land or on land not owned or controlled by themselves. *High value was placed on pursuits which did not involve manual work.* Within agriculture, the dominant productive activity provides the inverse relationship between the extent of manual work performed and the degree of control over the land.

The gradation in the village rested on a combination of economic inequality and inequality of status and found their concrete expression in the institution of caste. Prominent part is played by vertical ties of every kind, varying from the formal and elaborate pattern of 'Jajmani' system to the informal and variable relation between patron and client. There are two interrelated principles involved in relation to gradations in control over land on the one hand and on the other, to gradation in types of work on a scale of purity and pollution. The patron-client relationship i.e. vertical ties between landlord and tenant, between master and servant and between the creditor and debtor are not always necessarily channeled along the lines of caste. What kept the vertically arranged layers in their place were the many networks running up and down—and laterally—through which individuals and families are linked together. Patrons may have clients in their own castes as well as in other castes. Patron-client ties serve to bridge the cleavage between castes.

The Caste System is characterised by three features: hereditary specialization, hierarchial organization and mutual repulsion. Hereditary specialisation engenders narrowmindedness, nepotism, selfishness and other evils. *Hierarchial organization with religious sanction, being not based on democracy make the caste members religious fanatics having no personality to resist the unjust activities of the ruling authority.* In such organisation bereft of any free thinking there is no inquisitiveness about latest developments in modern world. Mutual repulsion is between different castes and sub-castes. Every caste considers it to be superior to some other castes.

The ideology behind the caste system breeds inequality and discrimination; *it teaches the higher castes to despise the members of lower castes.* As a result there is a general contempt for manual labour amongst the upper caste elites. *And this leads to bureaucracy of upper caste ruling class.*

Caste system nourishes resignation: puts a premium on conformity at the expense of personal initiative. One thinks himself as a member of a particular caste, rather than a member of the community. Social responsibility is thereby neglected. For example, a sweeper does not serve the community; he only serves the rule of upper castes and *his acceptance of his condition is not the acceptance of the social function but submission to hereditary debasement.* Non-resistance to injustice acts as an incentive for additional oppression.

The maintenance of the evil of caste system for centuries makes the individual feel that his social position has been preordained, determined by his birth and family connections. As a result he becomes a victim of pessimism, believing in inevitability of a life of miseries.

The pressure of the older generation is conservative; it corrupts the young. It tends to restrict initiative and perpetuate the existing structure of exploitation of men by men.

An individual who thinks of himself as a member of caste rather than a member of community can not possibly have the proper sense of neighbourhood; and it is the caste system which accounts for the state of insanitation. Only personal cleanliness needs to be observed with scrupulous attention to the taboos of pollution. Everybody, nursed by the caste complex takes it for granted that someone somehow will get rid of the refuse afterwards. *The caste system disintegrates responsibility; it does not diffuse it.*

The process of a low caste or tribe taking over the customs, rituals, belief, ideology and style of life of a high caste has been recognised by Prof. M.N. Srinivas as 'Sanskritization' which is primarily responsible for sustaining the caste system for about forty centuries. The concept was, however, first introduced by Prof. S.K. Chatterjee to characterise the nature of interaction between Vedic Aryans, pre-Aryan autochthones and the incoming non-Aryans.

A. Caste System in Rural Area:

Our villages have three characteristics, such as (1) system of multiple gradations, associated with an elaborate division of labour (2) innumerable vertical ties between families and individuals and (3) general acceptance of hierarchial values. Gradations in villages is seen most easily in terms of arrangement of castes and sub-castes. Typically the multicaste system has not only top and bottom but a number of intermediate layers.

Social life in a village is based mainly on an economy of land and grain. Apart from agriculture there are crafts and services of different kinds. Relation between these three determines the distinctive design of village organisation. When the relation undergoes change, the design becomes eroded. Everybody in the village might make a living from agriculture; land is the most valued reward for any kind of service. According to custom, some are required to abstain from all manual work, some to perform most onerous form of manual work and others whose customs allowed the men to work on farm, but not the women. *The manual workers in general are all of low castes or Untouchables.* Distinction between different grades in agricultural hierarchy are at one level structural but all peasants are not comparable to 'so many potatoes in a sack of potatoes'. Gradations in villages rested on a combination of economic inequalities and status inequalities; and finds the concrete expression in the institution of caste. However, *castes are not economically homogeneous.*

Vertical ties of every kind, range from the formal and elaborate pattern of 'jajmani' relations to informal and variable relations between patron and client. In the past, not only were different people unequally placed, but each knew where he belonged and was in a large measure, reconciled to his place in the total scheme of things. This contributed to the stability of the design that was distinctive of the village.

Hierarchial values were actively espoused only by those (upper caste people) at the top, while those at the bottom (low caste/ Untouchables) were merely reconciled to them. Hierarchial values are most clearly expressed through the traditional arrangement of castes, but they had some significance for every type of social categorisation involving superior and inferior positions. As a result not only Brahmans and Untouchables but also landowners and landless labourers are in some ways considered as destined to play unequal roles in life. A landlord is more than a mere landlord, when he is also a superior caste; conversely the landless are doubly deprived when they are also Untouchables. Priests, barbers, washerman and scavengers are unequally ranked not only by virtue of their work alone, but also because the castes to which they belong are unequally ranked. Tradition, religion and custom combine to sustain a moral environment in which hierarchy is considered to be part of the natural scheme.

Caste society is made up in such a way that the activity of an individual in the village is confined mostly to his own group. This is so particularly in relation to the social and cultural aspects. *The habitation area in each vlllage is divided in to areas containing houses of one particular caste*. Besides the caste clusters, the village is generally divided into two main habitation areas, one belonging to higher castes and the other to lower castes.

Friendships outside the caste group are not only rare in villages, but are generally accompanied by much shame and a feeling of guilt. *Sheltering in one's own house or nursing a sick person of a caste other than one's own is not possible.* However, as regards other activities, people borrow money from any caste and accept employment from any caste. Thus, only social activities are confined within the caste. There is no intercaste marriage while economic activities cut across the caste frontier.

The state of affairs in villages hinders the formation of political class forces because the principal exploited classes are themselves divided into a large number of castes and sub-castes. Each lower caste always tends to align with the upper castes/ sub-castes enjoying privileges.

In theory, the caste system does not lay down what work or profession a person shall take to but reserves access to certain occupation. For example, non-Brahmans are not allowed to act as priest or purohit. The close relationship between a person's caste and his occupation is due to the absence of or under-development of monetary economy in rural areas. Whereever monetary economy has been introduced, things have changed. In modern times, there has been some modifications in the occupational character of caste. For example, barbers, washermen, and carpenters, even in rural areas now openly express preference for the basis of cash payment. The 'jajmani' system is not operative now. The change from the system of exchange of goods and service to the system of monetary exchange permits a change in the technique, because it becomes possible to buy new production tools. The barbers, carpenters and blacksmiths now use machine-turned instruments and this acts as a good progressive trend.

B. Caste System in Urban Areas:

City life has completely undermined the foundation (economic) of the caste system. The system, however, though weakened, remains and its evil effects continue to vitiate the psyche of urban population in general. The social division of labour in cities and towns have been completely changed; traditional links between certain occupations and certain castes no longer exist. Thank to reservation for Scheduled Castes and Scheduled Tribes, there are now members of lower castes and out-castes even in the Parliament and Indian Administrative Services. However, the new hierarchy of occupational income does not differ from that of old hierarchy. Those placed by tradition high in the order of castes are often at the top of the scale even in cities and towns. The higher castes possessed either money or education or both and they took the lead in the new commercial administrative and industrial structures, whereas the lower castes, in general, were hampered by their lack of money and of education. As a result, *the new class structure in urban areas has not really replaced the old*; it has simply grown up upon the remains of the old frame-work. The distance between castes has not been bridged but the change has certainly shaken the foundation of the caste system. Another factor to weaken the system in urban areas is the weakening of the pressure (from caste panchayat) on the individuals belonging to the lower castes.

The pressure of older generation tends to reduce social mobility, restrain initiative and prepetuate the existing social order of exploitation. Such conditions are highly unfavourable to social and economic progress. *The principal reason why the caste system still survives in urban life is that it is still enforced in rural life.* Links between towns and village have not been broken. Factory workers in our country are out and out peasants in their mentality. Thus *agrarian reforms and newer farming techniques are as important as industrialization if the caste system is to disappear.*

People living in towns, cspecially the poorer classes have to defend their rights by community action; and the *caste system offers the simplest form of association.* This explains why caste spirit is strongest among the poorest section of the urban population. Caste system provides political parties with a readymade channel of communication and mobilisation; and consequently the importance of caste would increase in bourgeois parliamentary politics.

Even the industrial proletariat in urban areas are subject to a large extent, to the influence of caste. However, caste spirit is definitely weaker among factory workers as compared to rural peasantry.

In urban areas, new organisations based on membership of caste in question, particularly the Untouchables (dalits) are being formed. Such organisations promote caste spirit and thereby inculcate the vice of communalism. Thus the exploited toiling masses are being led astray and as a result the task of strengthening class unity becomes all the more difficult. To counter such organisations at the political level should be regarded as the primary task on the part of activists of revolutionary radical political parties.

Current Trends:

Regarding the persent position of the caste system, the Mandal Commission remarked. "Caste restrictions have loosened considerably as a result of the rule of law introduced by the British urbanisation, industrialistion and adult franchise. *But all the above changes mark only the shift in emphasis and not any material alteration of the basic structure of caste.* It is generally agreed that certain taboos have weakened as a result of all the above changes, *the importance of casteism in Indian politics is on the increase* . . . what caste has lost on ritual front, it has more than gained in political front. In view of this, it will be unrealistic to assume that the institution of caste will wither away in the foreseeable future". It is noteworthy that members of the opposition as well as treasury benches congratulated the Commission and bestowed their praise on its report. However, its modest recommendation of 27% reservation for members of 'Backward Classes' who constitute 52% of total population has not yet been accepted by the Government of India.

Within our society, during the period from the last quarter of 18th century upto the present the following changes occurred:

1. Increase in population and a state of scarcity of labour in relation to the cultivable land changed into a state of scarcity of land in relation to the availability of labour force.
2. Ownership of land was created and the position of certain categories in relation to land rights was drastically changed.
3. Land revenue became high and circulation of money increased.
4. Rapid means of communication and largescale transport were set up.
5. The importance of mercantile community increased considerably.
6. Food crops and commercial crops grew in importance.

All these above changes were analysed and Karl Marx (New York Daily Tribune, 25 June, 1853; 'On Colonialism', p. 33) remarked: "*England has broken down the entire framework of Indian Society*, without any symptoms of reconstitution yet appearing". He also wrote (ibid, 8 August, 1853; ibid p. 80): "*Modern industry, resulting from the railway system, will dissolve the hereditary division of labour, upon which rest the Indian Castes*". *There occurred a change in the society; not a change of the society*. Caste society managed to digest what was thought must make it asunder.

However, there had been the following changes in regard to the caste system: (a) Non-Brahman movement resulted in weakening of caste hierarchy (b) Notions concerning impurity has weakened (c) Rules concerning food and drink have been relaxed especially in towns (d) Freedom of new profession means that caste no longer prescribes occupation. But endogamy continue to hold sway with undiminished force.

In urban areas, castes group themselves by quarters, they have reserved houses, they create cooperatives, banks, maternity homes and general hospitals, and their associations. Caste associations are becoming more and more widespread whereas caste panchayats covered smaller areas-confined to limits of towns and villages. All these tend to engender new forms of solidarity and caste-spirit. Thus, *community aspects of caste has been made more comprehensive, extensive and permanent. More and more of an individual's self-interests are being catered for by caste.* The feeling of caste solidarity is a sort of caste patriotism.

Caste values are so deeply rooted in our society that modern ferments are unable to get a foot-hold in the psyche of even the young elites. Young men belonging to upper castes and to the most modernized strata of the society, subjected at the university to the full impact of western ideas, *are all essentially conservative.* Only a tiny minority of them are opposed to the joint family and traditional marriage. Life in our towns often remain rural in spirit. Thus, there has been a great increase in caste solidarity and the concomitant decrease of a sense of interdependence between different castes living in a region.

Now-a-days, caste associations rarely intervene in the everyday life of the villager. There is now an increased tension between different castes and *these tensions re-inforce caste solidarity.* Bourgeois politics reinforce the power of the caste, particularly at the time of the elections.

In caste system, politico-economic aspects are relatively secondary and isolated. It is significant that Brahmans, the leaders of caste society did not turn the 1857 mutiny into a holy war. The rise of non-landed capital of merchants and moneylenders did not arouse any reactions; the moneylender came to be known as 'mahajan' i.e. great man! Rabindranath Tagore (Sabuj Patra, November-December 1914) commented:

"Domination of Vaishyas has been established today. Trade and commerce are no longer trade and commerce now-they have been wedded secretly to empires. *There used to be a time when the Vaishyas owned only the commodities, now they own other men*".

In our society, once the dominance of Brahman ideology is accepted, the political power is granted to any individual irrespective of his caste status; because such individual can be assimilated into the ruling clique of upper caste Hindus. A Jagjivan Ram or a Damodaran Sanjeevaiah who surrendered to the Brahman ideology could rise to high position. Dr. Ambedkar had been a true rebel against Brahman ideology of Kautilyan culture. He did not compromise with the upper caste Hindu political leaders in the garb of 'Mahatma' or 'Socialist'. It must be remembered that *the political roots of caste lie in Kautilyan culture based on the principle of 'Divide and Rule'*.

Kautilya advised the King: "Senior members of the tribe should be encouraged not to eat at the tribal common table (eka-patram) or intermarry with the lesser who in turn were to be egged on to insist upon meals in common and intermarriage. Recognised status within the tribe was to be upset by every sort of internal provocation. Royal agents could needle the younger people, who are allotted a minor share of tribal lands and revenue by custom, to question the apportionment. *The leaders and the most active tribal clements were to be corrupted by castc/tribes, ample supplies of the strongest wines, secret agents, Baahmans and astrologers, women apparently of good lineage, dancers, actors, singers and harlots* . . . Murder of tribcsmen by ambush or poison, for which the blame would be put upon known rivals within the tribe and rumours that chiefs had been rumours that chiefs had bcen bribed by the enemy would also help lead to open clashes. Then the king of the Arthasastra state would intervene directly with armed forces. The tribe was to be fragmented, the tribesmen deported, to be settled upon distant lands in units of five to ten households well away from each other so that they should not be able to master tactical manoevres in the field-movements and intentions of the savages would be spied out by special agents, usually distinguished as hermits, if too powerful but nevertheless ripe to change to food production, the forest-tribes could be subverted by the methods explained above". (Kosambi, D.D.—'The culture and civilisation in ancient India').

All Hindu rulers used Arthashastra – the political treatise authored by Kautilya as their political handbook. Kautilya's principle of Dharma revolves round the maintenance of political and ideological supremacy of the two upper varnas – Brahmans and Kshatriyas and also complete segregation of Shudra Varna into several caste groups so that their unity becomes impossible. If we compare Kautilya's culture to that of the Muslim and British rulers, there would be little to choose; *Kautilyan culture is probably more conspiratorial and brutal.*

Kautilyan political line began to operate in a very sophisticated manner following the transfer of political power to INC. Constitutionally caste as an institution has been abolished and the aim of republic is declared to be the establishment of casteless and classless society! But in reality, at every level, structures have been created and measures undertaken to strengthen the caste system. Adventitious aids to Untouchables and Backward castes, reservation have been provided knowing fully well that employment and education to an extremely small section of the downtrodden would only nurture casteism in offices and educational institutions. The government have not done anything in the direction of eliminating backwardness (social, educational and economic) of the low caste Untouchables. Their level of consciousness has been maintained so low that they started believing that the 'fortunate' and 'competent' among them would get dignified job and higher education. The 'fortunate' and 'competent low' caste/Untouchables are the few hand-picked individuals who; rather inadvertantly are transformed into agents of Brahman ideology. As a result, solidarity amongst the low caste/Untouchables become weaker, while the camp of upper caste ruling class becomes stronger. Weakening of caste solidarity is a gain because caste consciousness is false consciousness, an ideological mode of subjugating the low castes/Untouchables and this has to be combated to hasten its demise.

In the advocacy of meritocracy and urge to usher in 'silicon culture', the ruling elites would be quite content, if necessary, to leave more than half the population below the poverty line. In this context the stoking of communal passions and casteist sentiment is an attempt to divide the people and coopt the majority community to protect privileges of the middle class without having to share the economic cake with them. The most potent threat at the moment is the communal manoevring of the state. The answer should be grassroot mobilization of the exploited and oppressed masses who are mostly low caste/ Untouchables.

7

Magnitude of the Caste Problem

Nowhere in the world had there been any society with stratification into castes and subcastes as in our Hindu society in which about a quarter of its total members were subjected to the most inhuman oppression. Dr. B.R. Ambedkar, who had been the most important leader of the Untouchables remarked "*Hindu civilization produced 5 crores of Untouchables, some 2 crores of tribal people and some 50 thousand criminal tribes people*".

Tyranny of caste system, experienced by him in his early life is as follows: when he was only 5 years old, he learnt that no barber would cut his hair for fear of pollution and so this chore had to be done by his sister. Stranded with his sister on the railway piatform at Gurgaon, he found that no bullock cart driver would take them. And when he found one cart, the driver would not drive the cart, a job he had to do it himself. Finally they had to drink water which was full of dirt and dung. Returning from England, with a Doctorate degree to serve the Baroda state according to the terms of scholarship he availed, Ambedkar found that no one was willing to rent a house to him. Taking a false name Adalji Sorabji he took refuge in a Parsee Dharamshala. But there was no respite here too. A mob of Parsee youngmen armed with lathis accosted him and threatened to kill him, demanding to know who he was. He had to leave this place also, and unable to find any other place, went back to Bombay.

The 'Untouchable's according to Hutton (Caste in India), were originally designated as 'exterior caste' in British India and they were subjected to a number of prohibitions. These were as follows:

1. Adi-Dravida and Devendrakula Velalars should not wear clothes below knees;
2. They should not wear jewels of gold;
3. Their women should carry water only in earthen pots;
4. They should work as slaves of Mirasdars;
5. They should not cultivate land of either varam or lease from Mirasdars;
6. Their children should not read and get them literate;
7. Their children should tend cattle of Mirasdars.
8. They must sell away their own lands to Mirasdars. *Even if something grows by the help of rain water, crops should be* robbed away;
9. They must work as coolies from 7 A.M. to 6 P.M. under Mirasdar and wage is Rs. 0-4-0 per day and for female Rs. 0-2-0.
10. They should not use Indian music at their marriage ceremony;
11. They must stop the habit of going on horse in procession before tying the Thali thread in marriages.

In Kerala, elaborate rules had been laid down requiring the minimum distance that should prevail between the various castes. J H. Hutton has quoted the following passage from "The Anthropology of Nayaddis" by A. Aiyappan; pp. 18 ff.

"Aiyappan in 1937, gives a scale of distance pollution for several castes; a Nayar must keep 7 feet from a Nambudri Brahman, an Iravan (Illavan, Izhavan, Tiyan) must keep 32, a Cheruman, 64 and a Nayadi 74 to 124. The respective distances between these lower castes are calculated by a simple process of subtraction; the Iravan must keep 25 feet from the Nayar and Cheruman 32 feet from the Iravan.

Even today, some prohibitions like qualitative restrictions on consumption and on behaviour are very much prevalent in rural areas. For example, the lower castes of Bihar faced restrictions, like, not walking through upper caste bastis wearing footwear or carrying umbrella. Sitting on a cot in the presence of upper caste landowner/moneylender had been unthinkable. *Upper caste names also were taboo for the lower castes*; the Untouchables had perforce to have names like Dukhi Ram and so on.

In the more than decade long agrarian movements in Bihar, the dignity of the people of lower castes including Untouchables has been asserted. The simplest rights, the city people take for granted, were not earlier available to them in the villages. *There are innumerable instances of people being beaten up for daring to wear clean clothes or brightly coloured sweater.* The subjugation of low castes was most apparent and cruel in the case of low caste/Untouchable women. Though in the 'dola' tradition (doli carrying the newly married girl stopping first at the landlord's house) is a matter of the past, yet women of lower castes till recently, generally were forced to sexually submit to men of the upper caste. As recently as the late 1970's, the Untouchables of Bihar were subjected to various indignities mentioned above. In Bihar, 'holi' represented directly the subjugation of lower caste women in particular. With the Untouchables now organised, many aspects of holi had been changed; *upper caste men no longer dare molest lower caste women or sing songs about them.* Notwithstanding their numerical preponderance, low caste Hindu population, particularly in rural areas continue to remain in bondage of the high caste landowners and money lenders. The big bourgeoisie, being comprador in nature. are interested to maintain the semi-feudal or pre-capitalist production relation in agriculture.

The ban on contact between castes/subcastes and the solidarity of a subcaste are manifested in the spatial segregation of castes in villages. The Untouchables must live everywhere at some distance from others, while each subcaste occupies a street or a quarter of the town or village.

The acceptance of cooked food from an Untouchable by an upper caste individual constitute serious offence and in old days such offence was punished with excommunication from the caste.

Some occupations are considered defiling because of the contact with some defiling object. Swine-herding is defiling because swine defile. Leather defiles and consequently the making and repairing of shoes is an occupation of the Untouchables. Certain other occupations while not being defiling, are so strongly associated with low castes that no upper caste man would take to them. Any occupation, however, remotely implying the destruction of life in any form would be prohibited to the upper castes. Butchery, catching of fish and game and the raising of sheep and fowl are prohibited. Even the selling of dried fish and eggs are regarded as an improper occupation for upper caste Hindu.

There are as many as sixty six lakh men and women (mostly women) who still *carry human excreta on the head, often in leaking buckets and nobody seem to be interested in abolishing this abominal practice* forced on the Untouchables (scavengers). Scavenging is a blot on our culture; it violates the U.N. Charter on Human Rights.

In 1956, the "Zamindari" system has been abolished but in Bihar 40% of the land area in a village is still owned by a

Zamindar. The land-lord of Dumras, Hatia. Karsilla of Bihar are even now owners of thousands of acres of cultivable land. Maharaja of Darbhanga currently stand at the third position as the payer of property tax. *There are about 10,000 'Mohants'* who own huge land area under cultivation. It has been estimated that 80% of peasants together own a total of 5% of cultivable land whereas the rest 20% own as much as 80% of land area. In Bihar there are SC 14.11%, ST 8.75% and OBC's 47.18% and almost all of them are toiling manual workers. Along with the development of capitalism in agricultural production there arose a new class of Kulaks and moneylenders and they belong to the *intermediate castes of Yadavs, Kurmis, Keoris* etc. They constitute only 18.5% of OBC's and of them only 8.5% are prosperous. Thus if the remaining OBC's are added to SC and ST, the total would amount to 61.5% of the total population. Most of them are either poor peasants or landless agricultural labourers belonging to low castes/Untouchables; they have to suffer not only economic exploitation but also atrocities at the hands of upper and intermediate caste landowners/money lenders.

Issue of Untouchables and Backward Castes is the issue of the cultivable land. Situation in the villages is horrible. Feudal exploitation is devastating; the peasantry are turning into more and more landless agricultural labourers. According to Govt. Statistics, the break-up of the various categories in rural areas of Andhra Pradesh is as follows:

Category	*Number of Households*
Agricultural households (including landless labourers)	41,21,000
Agricultural labourers	15,37,000
Handicrafts and other professions	10,18,000
Landless and without any profession	6,51,000
Total	73,27,000

It is to be noted that there are many agricultural labourers amongst the last two categories. In fact, it is due to the pressure of increasing number of landless agricultural labourers, wage rates have fallen.

Most of the people living in the rural areas have lost their land in the course of feudal exploitation. Today, they have nothing but their hands to make ends meet. To them, except in areas where cash crops like sugar cane developed, it is a great thing if they can get work for more than six months in a year. They have to sustain themselves for the whole year with the earnings of those six months. Over half of the agricultural labourers are located in the wet land areas where paddy is the main crop and the rest in the dry land areas. Most of these families may be able to eat at least once a day during the working season but it is no exaggeration to say that they stay half dead with little food in the agricultural off-season that lasts for a minimum of 4 months. In Andhra Pradesh, a major proportion of these agricultural labourers belong to the scheduled castes like Mala, Maliga, Netakani, Dekkali, Mastinu, Gurram, Desari, Sindhu, Baindle etc. Their huts are situated in hamlets known in Telugu as 'gudem' which stays thrown out of the main village boundary; although government records show their gudem as part of the villages. The Untouchables, in fact. remain outcastes banished from participation in the village social life. Nevertheless, the Untouchables have to go daily into the village in order to work. *But they can not roam wearing chappals in the market frequented by the forward caste people*! They can not go under umbrellas in front of upper caste people even in blazing summers! They are not allowed to drink water from the village wells used by other castes. The backward castes rank second among the agricultural labourers after the Malas and Maligas. They belong to various castes like Golla (Shepherd), Chakali (washerman), Mangali (barber), Kumar (potter), Gowda (toddy tapper), Mudiraju, Tenugu, Mannur, Kapu etc. Unlike Malas and Maligas, they live within the village. At one time they held different vocations but most of the vocations got destroyed in the course of time. Today most of them depend on agricultural labour and they are landless. A small proportion of them may own a little land but agricultural labour is the main occupation.

Apart from these Untouchables and Backward Castes, some Scheduled Tribes like Erukala, Yenadi, Lambadi etc. who live in villages also work as agricultural labourers.

Among all these kinds of agricultural labourers there are some who belong to the categories of poor and even middle peasants, too. However, most of them, in addition to working in their own land, also work as labourers in other's fields. The combine of landless agricultural labourers, poor peasants and middle peasants comprise about 70% of the rural population. The castes like Brahman, Vaishya, Reddi, Kamma, Kapur, Velama, Kshatriya, Kalinga etc. are considered as forward castes. They constitute the majority of land owners in Andhra Pradesh.

Forward castes like Reddy, Kamma, Kapu, Valama, Kshatriya, Kalinga etc. are primarily agricultural castes. Most of the landlords belong to these castes who enjoy the highest social status in the rural areas where the power is concentrated in their hands. *After the end of British rule, political power gradually changed hands from Brahmans to these landed classes.* Big landlords of these castes have become the ruling class of the State government.

Forward castes also have a good number of poor people among their ranks. However, by virtue of their kinship as well as various other constraints, they are always inclined to be under the patronage of landlords. They think that such patronage is their security against many problems which, in fact, is far from truth. They are used by the landlords as their henchmen when needed but they get nothing in return. They are always exploited.

Thus class relations and class contradictions are strongly emerging between the castes and also within the castes. The relation between the backward castes/Untouchable and forward castes manifest as relations and contradictions between the poor and the rich or the exploiter and the exploited. Therefore, the caste issue is also proving to be a class issue, in essence.

The magnitude of the problem of caste stratification with the associated socio-political consequences can be appreciated from the following tables provided by the Backward Class Commission set up by the Government of India.

TABLE 1

Percentage Distribution of Indian Population by Caste and Religious Groups

Group Name	*Percentage of total population*
1. Scheduled Castes and Scheduled Tribes	
(i) Scheduled Castes	15.05
(ii) Scheduled Tribes	7.51
Total	22.56
2. Non-Hindu Communities, Religious Goups etc.	
(i) Muslims (Other than STs)	11.19 (0.02)
(ii) Christian (Other than STs)	2.16 (0.44)
(iii) Sikhs (Other than SC/ST)	1.67 (0.22)
(iv) Buddhists (Other than STs)	0.67 (0.03)
(v) Jains	0.47
Total	16.16

3. Forward Hindu Castes and Communities.	5.52
Brahmans (including Bhumihars) Rajputs	3.90
Marathas	2.21
Jats	1.00
Vaishyas-Bania etc.	1.88
Kayasthas	1.07
Other Forward Hindu/Castes/Groups	2.00
Total	17.58
4. Backward Hindu Castes and Communities which comes in the category of OBCs*	43.70
5. Backward non-Hindu communities	8.40
6. The approximate population of OBCs* including non-Hindu communities	52%

Figures in brackets give population of SC/ST among non-Hindu communities.

*Other Backward Class.

TABLE 2

Repesentation of SC, ST and Other Backward Classes, in Central Govt. Services

	Cass I			Class II		
	Total	*SC/ST*	*OBC*	*Total*	*SC/ST*	*OBC*
1. Ministries/ Departments	11,707	840 (7.18)	303 (2.59)	43,803	5.985 (13,66)	1,742 (3,98)
2. Autonomous bodies Attached and sub-ordinate offices	81,325	5,399 (6.64)	4.147 (5.09)	503,337	91,431 (18.16)	59,079 (11.74)
3. Public Sector Undertakings	80,994	3,652 (4.51)	3,719 (4.59)	365,785	68,566 (18.74)	36,242 (9.91)
4. Total	174,026	9 891 (5.68)	8,169 (4.69)	912,925	165,982 (18.18)	97,063 (10.63)

Note: Figures in brackets represent percentagcs.

Representation of SC/ST and Other Backward Classes in Central Government Services

Class III			*Class IV*		
Total	*SC/ST*	*OBC*	*Total*	*SC/ST*	*OBC*
17,829	5,518	1,500	73,339	12,343	3,545
	(30.95)	(8.41)		(16.83)	(4.83)
322,948	67,118	67,786	907.610	163,748	131,012
	(20.78)	(20.98)		(18.06)	(14.43)
143,910	45,646	22,689	590,689	117,869	62,650
	(31.72)	(15.77)		(19.95)	(10.61)
484,687	118,282	91,975	1571,638	294,155	197,267
	(24.40)	(18.98)		(18.72)	(12.55)

TABLE 3

Political and Administrative Officers at the Highest Level (1980)

Posts	*Total Number*	*Number of Brahmans alone*
Governor/Lt. Governor	27	13
Secretary to Governor/ Lt. Governor	24	13
Union Cabinet Ministers	19	10
Chief Secretaries to State Governments	26	14
Private Secretaries to Ministers	49	34
Secretary/Addl. Secretary/Jt. Secretary and equivalents at the Centre	500	310 (Approx)
Vice-Chancellors	98	50
Supreme Court Judges	16	9
High Court Judges/Addl. HCJ	330	166
Ambassadors/High Commissioners	140	58
Chief Executive Public Sector Undertakings:		
Central	158	91
State	17	14

TABLE 4

Number of Brahmans in the Parliament

	1952	*1957*	*1962*	*1967*	*1971*	*1977*	*1980*
Lok Sabha							
Proportion of Brahman number	173/ 499	230/ 490	210/ 510	192/ 523	178/ 523	136/ 542	100/ 530
Rajya Sabha	*1952*	*1957*	*1960*	*1964*	*1968*	*1970*	*1974*
Proportion	70/ 216	108/ 232	115/ 236	102/ 238	104/ 230	113/ 238	112/ 240
						1978	*1980*
						84/ 244	89/ 244

NB.: In 1931, the Brahmans in India totalled 155 lakhs out of a total population of 3505 lakhs, i.e. only 4.41%. Taking into account the increase in the percentage population of Hindus as a result of Partition, the percentage of Brahmans would stand at 5.40 or so. From the above two tables, it is indicated that Brahmans held more than 50% of Government offices at the highest level and also in the Parliament.

TABLE 5

Election of SC and ST to non-reserved seats in Lok Sabha

Election Year	*Total Seats*	*Reserved for SC*	*Reserved for ST*	*Non-Reserved*	*Non-Reserved Filled by SC*	*Non-Reserved Filled by ST*
1952	489	72	24	392	5 (1)	1 (0)
1957	494	76	31	387	7 (3)	3 (2)
1962	494	76	31	387	2	2
1967	520	77	36	407	0	1
1971	522	77	40	405	1	4
1977	542	78	38	426	2	1

TABLE 6

Election of SC and ST to non-reserved seats in Vidhan Sabhas

Election Year	*Total Seats*	*Reserved for SC*	*Reserved for ST*	*Non-Res.*	*Non-Res. Filled by SC*	*Non-Res. Filled by ST*
1952	3234	471	192	2571	5	2
1957	3201	470	221	2411	7	9
1962	3206	480	262	2553	12	13
1967	3467	496	248	2723	4	8
1975-77	3977	540	282	3155	Nil	Nil

8

Atrocities on Scheduled Castes and Scheduled Tribes

It is well known that atrocities committed on SC and ST people have social and economic causes at the root. The social cause lies in the practice of untouchability which is a by-product of the caste system. The social disability or backwardness is further re-inforced by economic factors like land disputes, forcible harvesting of crops and dispute over payment of wages to landless agricultural labourers. Other factors like provision of house sites and other development schemes aimed at amelioration of socio-economic conditions of Scheduled Caste people also cause discontentment among the privileged Caste-Hindus which lead to clashes among the two sections. The situation is further aggravated by the fact that SC people are now demanding social and economic equality with the upper caste Hindus.

Atrocities on Scheduled Tribe people are principally committed by the landlords, money lenders and the police. Land alienation, indebtedness. forest policy restricting the interests of the tribals in the forest, changing excise policy against poor tribals, non-payment of minimum wages, bonded labour, charging of excess toll tax by the 'Hat' lesses from the tribals and exploitation by local forest officials, police and non-tribal people are the main reasons of atrocities on ST people.

State government have identified the following districts which are sensitive from the point of view of crimes against SC people.

1. Bihar—Patna, Nalanda, Rohtas, Bhojpur, Gaya, Vaishali, Samastipur, Begusarai, Bhagalpur, Mongyr and Ranchi.
2. Gujarat—Ahmedabad, Mehsena. Surenuanagar, Junagarh, Kheda, Amreli, Rajkot, Banskanta, Vedodara, Varneh and Kutch.
3. Haryana—Ambala, Karnal, Sonepat, Gurgaon, Faridabad.
4. Karnataka—Bangalore, Bijapur, Kolar, Mysore, Tumkur Gulbarga.
5. Madhya Pradesh—Morena, Bilaspur, Panna, Raipur, Jabalpur, Ujjain, Bhopal.
6. Maharashtra—Aurangabad, Bead, Osmanabad, Nanded, Parbhani, Buldana.
7. Punjab—2 villages in Ferozpur District, 3 villages in Sangrur District, 3 villages in Patiala District.

Names of Districts identified as sensitive from the point of view of crimes against Scheduled Tribe people.

1. Bihar—Singhbhum, Lohardanga, Palamau, Ranchi, Dumka, Sahibganj, Dhanbad, Hazaribagh, Giridhi and Godda.
2. Maharashtra—Dhule, Nasik, Jalgaon, Osmanabad, Parbhani, Chandrapur, Gad-chiroli, Bhandara, and Amaravati.

Crimes against scheduled caste people increased in a number of states over the years, as is evident from statistics of crimes against SC under IPC during the years 1982, 1983 and 1984 (Committee on welfare of SC and ST: 1985-86). The total number of crimes against Scheduled Tribe people also increased in the States of Madhya Pradesh, Rajasthan, Bihar, Maharashtra and Gujarat. The Committee regretted that *the number of offenders aequitted is far more than the offenders convicted in the cases of crimes committed against SC people.* For example, in 1982, 1483 persons were convicted and 2422 acquitted; in 1984, 1450 were convicted whereas 1851 acquitted; The Committee noted that the state of U.P. where the number of cases of crime against SC peeople is highest (13, 692 in 1982, 14,734 in 1983 and 12,063 in 1984) have not set up any special court to expedite the disposal of cases. The number of cases of crime against SC people pending in the Court in 1982 were 23,662 which had risen to 26,261 in 1984. According to Peoples Unioh for Democratic Rights (PUDR) in Bihar, during January, 1980 to October, 1986 as many as *390 Harijans have been killed as victims of caste/class tyranny.*

Disabilities of SC and ST poeple can be roughly divided into two categories. First, that under which they are debarred from public utilities, such as the use of roads and tanks, and secondly, their religious disabilities which debar them from the use of temples, burning ghats, and some other institutions. In addition to above, but arising out of the second of these, there are the disabilities involved in the relationship of private individuals.

Resolution of the Anti-Untouchability Conference of 1929 in Madras regretted to note that in restaurants, coffee hotels, hair-dressing saloons, water pandals etc. notices are hung prominently excluding the Untouchables, and the Census Superintendent for the Central Provinces wrote: "The fact that a sweeper may sit beside a high-class Hindu in a railway carriage or motor lorry without any question of his right to do so has not yet made it any more easy in the interior for a touring officer to persuade cartmen of some castes to carry his sweeper from camp to camp. In fact, in certain districts it is always essential to employ at least one cartman of humble caste for this purpose".

Apart from the above disabilities which are nothing but atrocious restrictions, there are cases of non-implementation of the rights granted by the Constitution. Even though there are seats in the Parliament (Lok Sabha) as well as in State Assemblies (Vidhan Sabhas); reserved the number of seats reserved for SC and ST are not commensurate with the number of these Untouchables. This is particularly so in case of ST poeple.

Moreover, *very few SC and ST people have so far been elected in the non-reserved seats.* The two tables (5 and 6) illustrate that the stigma of 'Untouchable' is very deep-rooted. Babu Jagjivan Ram was reported to have said that it would take more than 1000 years for an Untouchable to become the President of Indian Republic. Probably a wrong prophecy.

The low caste Shudras and Untouchables had to suffer not only economic exploitation but also social oppression. James Forbes (Oriental Memories, Vol. I 1834) wrote: If a Nayyar comes across a Puliya in a broad road, he used to unhesitatingly kill him as we can kill a lower animal. Raginald Graddock (The Dilemma in India, 1929) wrote: "In 1929 while giving evidence as witness to the Lee Commission at Madras, *the Untouchables were not allowed entry to the court room*, they had to speak from a distance outside the court room". Following are the few examples of social oppression by the Upper Caste Hindus on the Untouchables. These practices are no longer rigidly observed.

(1) In the Maratha country, a Mahar (Untouchable) might not spit on the road lest pure caste-Hindu should be polluted by touching it with his foot; he has to carry an earthen pot, hung from his neck, in which to spit. Further he had to drag a thorny branch with him to wipe out his footprints and to lie at a distance prostrate on the ground if a Brahman passed by, so that his foul shadow might not defile the holy Brahman. (Caste and Class in India – Ghurya).

(2) In Mysore State, the women of certain lower castes were not permitted to cover their bossoms. There arose a sharp controversy-over this issue resulting in civil disturbances and

ultimately the Maharaja of Mysore had to issue a royal proclamation permitting the aggrieved castes to wear jackets or cover their bossoms, in any manner they desire, but that *they were not permitted to imitate the dress and hair styles of higher castes.* (Social Movements and Social Transformation—M.S. Rao).

The award of punishments and levy of taxes were also related to one's caste. A Brahman was exempt from the usual taxes and private property were inviolate. In fact, *Kautilya prescribed differential rates of interests for debts according to different castes.* According to Manu "Slaying of Shudra by a Brahman is equivalent merely to the killing of a cat, a mangoose, a blue jay, a frog, a lizard, an owl or a crow". According to 'Satpatha Brahmana', a murder of a Brahman alone is the real murder". The above account will show as to how every important fact of a low caste Hindu's personal, social and economic activity was influenced by his low caste status.

In the 7th Lok Sabha, Prof. Madhu Dandavate cited an example of blind priestly prejudice against Untouchables: When Lord Mountbatten had invited Dr. B.R. Ambedkar, a member of his Executive Council to accompany him to a visit to Jagannath Puri temple, *the local priests happily welcomed Mountbatten to enter the temple, whereas they refused permission to Dr. Ambedkar!*" Regarding social status accorded to low castes, J.R. Kamble (Rise and Awakening of Depressed Classes in India) quoted the following passage from the 'Hindu' of 24.12.1932 as an example of *visual pollution*: "In this (Tinnevelly) district, there is a *class of unseeables called 'purada vannans'*. They are not allowed to come out during daytime because their sight is considered to be pollution! Some of these people who wash the clothes of other exterior castes working between midnight and daybreak, were with difficulty persuaded to leave their houses to interviews". It is hoped that such cases are not existent now. However, even now, Untouchables are denied the right to enter temples in South India, including Rajasthan and are subjected to multiple indignities.

In regard to atrocities on SC and ST people, Swanati Rao, the Deputy Minister for Social Welfare of Government of India said in Parliament in a written reply: In all, 13,519 incidents were reported in States in 1987 involving atrocities on Scheduled Castes. The total number of such cases reported was 15,403 and 15,373 in 1986 and 1985. As for atrocities on Scheduled Tribes 2,603 cases were reported in 1987 against 3,953 in 1986 and 4,055 in 1985. In these incidents, *595 Scheduled Caste and 90 Tribe people were kiled in 1987.* (Statesman 6.12.1988).

Minister of State Rajendra Kumari Bajpai informed the Rajya Sabha (Vide Statesman dt. 5.8.89) that Uttar Pradesh reported the highest number of cases of atrocities against SC people during the year 1988: 4,755 cases of atrocities against SC by non-SC were reported, which included 27 murders and 238 rape cases. As regards atrocities against ST by non-ST, Madhya Pradesh had the first place with a total of 2051, cases. These included 68 murders and 202 rapes. On 14th August, 1989, she told the Lok Sabha; "During 1988-89, a total of over 15,000 such cases of serious nature against SC members were registered and over 3,000 cases involving ST members. The Government is concerned at this disturbing trend" (Hindustan Times, 15th August 1989). She also said "Even cases of rape and minor offences against SC members totalled 3,300 and against ST members 783. We consider these not as isolated cases but as representing resistance to the changes taking place in the country . . . Since such atrocities offending human dignity has continued despite restrictive provisions against such practices in the Indian Penal Code and other laws, we have brought forward this comprehensive bill". The Government, according to the Minister, has decided that a permanent solution to the problem of atrocities on Scheduled castes and Scheduled Tribes lies in preventing such incidents than in taking corrective action. However, she did not spell out the precise method of prevention.

'Sunday (dated 5.11. Feb. 1989)' Statesman reported the killing of a young couple for intercaste marriage. The Rajput girl married a Punjabi boy and the girl's two brothers are alleged to be the killers. The father of girl says: "We are Rajputs; we do not allow even our sons to have intercaste marriages and you are talking about a daughter who has disgraced the Rajput community?" The Police Superintendent of Karnal says "we have arrested the accused, but *nobody is willing to depose as witness*". Such is the position of the caste problem.

The press is now-a-days full of news about brutal atrocities—rape of women, killing of women and children, particularly in Bihar. Analysis of massacare in the district of Jahanabad leads to the conclusion that the police-politician-landowner axis is involved. The private armies of landowners such as Bhoomisena (Kurmi Caste) Lorik Sena (Yadav Caste) and Brahmarshi Sena (Bhoomihar Caste) terrorise the poor Scheduled Caste agricultural labourers, rape their women and kill them and children enmasse in broad daylight. Massacres of Parasbigha, Arwal, Kansara, and Nonhi-Nagwal are all examples of atrocities on Scheduled Castes who were organised in MKSS and IPF. Landlords, criminals and the police came to develop an identity of interests against the SC agricultural labourers because they began to force landlords to pay government announced minimum wages and refused to part with ceiling surplus land, to fight social evils like dowry and alcoholism (forced the closure of liquor shops and distillaries) thereby offending interests of landlords, criminals and the police.

Government waste land and ceiling lands have been allotted by the Government to SC and ST and disputes arising out of it is the principal cause of atrocities on them. In a very large number of cases there has been dispossession of SC/ST from the lands allotted to them. In spite of the fact that most of the State governments have enacted legislation to stop transfer of tribal land to non-tribals. Large scale transfers of tribal land to non-tribals have taken place in the States of AndhraPradesh, Bihar, Gujarat, Karnataka, Madhya Pradesh, Maharashtra,

Orissa, Tripura and Uttar Pradesh. Obviously, legislations are not fool-proof and the rich people have taken advantage of such lacuna for grabing tribal land.

Non-payment of minimum wages is the other important cause of atrocities on poor scheduled caste/scheduled tribe agricultural labourers. Whenever they try to assert their right to get minimum wages fixed by the law they are threatened and atrocities are perpetrated on them. Unless the enforcement machinery for implementation of Minimum Wages Acts is adequately strengthened, atrocities on SC/ST will continue. In Bihar, most of crimes perpetrated against SC are caused by disputes over payment of wages to landless agricultural labourers, Atrocities on Scheduled Tribes are principally committed by landlord, moneylenders and the police.

There are two causes for the increasing number of crimes in Bihar against SC, perperated by the newly rich land owners/ moneylenders, During seventies, 89.9% of the total population of the State were rural. Moreover, *compared to 69.67% of the total population of India being engaged in agricultural activities, the percentage in Bihar was 82%*. Pradhan H. Prasad (Economic and Political Weekly' June 14, 1975) has shown that the average monthly income in Bihar was only two thirds of that in the country as a whole. According to Pranab Bardhan's estimate, since sixties, in the villages of Bihar, the number of people below the poverty line (monthly income less than Rs. 15/-) had been increasing as follows; in 1960-61, it was 37.64%, in 1964-65 it rose to 42.80% and *in 1967-68 it reached 80.65%*. Thus, the economic condition of the rural population of Bihar, who were mostly Untouchables was precarious; it was almost a famine.

In Bhojpur District of Bihar, there is a class of people known as 'Banihar'. According to caste, Doshad, Mushahar and Chamar constitute the majority of Banihars; and of them Mushahars are the poorest. They traditionally work as serfs under the landlord, rich peasants, sharecropper and 'batlidar's. They are given some land which is known as Katha land. In exchange they remain in bondage under these masters and have to carry out whatever work ordered by the latter. In recent years, Katha land area had been reduced in size from 1 bigha to 14 kathas. The amount of Doja was also reduccd. The gift of katha land for sugarcane and free food (nasta) was withdrawn. In addition, the serfs were compelled to guard land produce and carry the same to owner's house; no remuneration was granted for this additional work. Exploitation was markedly intensified; and there was revolt against it. Even B.N. Sinha, the Police Chief remarked: "The cry for land, treatment of equity and recognition of dignity of every man and woman is vociferous". Obviously, the oppression was primarily economic; secondarily based on caste.

The book "Bhojpur, Naxalism in Plains of Bihar" mentions about the landowner Bhumihar, by caste who complained about Jagadish Mahato, Kueri by caste: "He would often remark to his father Sudama, your son is not like you. You are his father and we have been your master for so many years. He thinks that because he can read and write, it is not necessary to respect his elders. Now-a-days, he does not get up from his seat from his cot in our presence. This is not right". Rahul Sankrityayan described the condition in Bihar villages: "In those villages where there are big Zamindars, it is difficult for a woman to defend her honour. Some of them have maintained some peasant families as serfs serving their masters. The serfs satisfied their hunger with left-over food of the master, they had to be on their legs from dawn to night."

The prowess and varna-prestige of the landowner, in the ultimate analysis, is based on their military power. In Bhojpur district, the number of licenced guns with Zamindars is 8,000. Caste tyranny or rape of women in Bihar is only incidental, the basic question is which class has established political power by what method. In the District of Bhojpur, atrocities on Untouchables are not crimes based on caste consideration.

Caste and class do not always converge. Examples are: Sheela Chatterji is a Brahman but to Untouchables there she is "Jhansi-Ka-Rani". Chandrika Singh is a Rajput but he is poor; he joined his own class. Without hesitation he has forshaken association with his caste brethern. In 1977, the President of the Committee for the suppression of Naxalities was a Harijan or untouchable Ramgidh Ram and the Secretary was Rajput, Deepti Singh. Rajdeo Ram is a Harijan but rich and an M.L.A. and so was an enemy to Naxalbari uprising. In Bhojpur, the battle against oppression and exploitation had been conducted simultaneously against caste and class. Bourgeois journalist tends to portray the struggles in Bihar as caste wars but in *reality these are class wars*.

Tyranny of upper caste landlord despots in Bihar villages is vividly portrayed in the Bengali novel 'Dhnorai charit-manas' by Satinath Bhaduri: a Scheduled Caste landless labourer had to appear before the tyrant in a position of standing on one leg! A Yadav, irrespective of his old age has to salute a child of the landlord family and the latter addresses thc former as 'Tu'! In Tamilnadu village of North Arcot district, people of Scheduled Caste cannot wear the Pagri or headgear. The worst form of tyranny is the rape of low caste/Scheduled caste women by the upper caste landlords. This aspect of caste oppression has been described with details in the book 'Bhojpur, Naxalism in the plains of Bihar' written by Kalyan Mukherji and Rajendra Singh Yadav. However, both Swami Sahajananda and Pandit Rahul Sankrityayan have pointed out that *such tyranny should be seen in the context feudal exploitation*. Rahulji wrote: "in the village having big Zamindar, it is difficult for the women of that village to defend or preserve their 'ijjat' (chastity). Some Zamindars have compelled some peasant families to become their 'servant of the Guru'. All men and women of these families are engaged for the life time as servants of the 'Babu'. Their condition was in no way better than 'das-dasi' (slaves). They had to survive depending on left-over food of the master. . . they had to work from dawn to late night, all the time being on legs."

Generally speaking, political power of a bourgeois state is based on the strength of millitary and police force; but in our villages the Zamindar has his own instrument of domination which is, however, supplemented by the local police force and other government employees. According to official records, there are as many as 8000 guns in the hands of Zamindars of Bhojpur district and they have about 50,000 armed gondas under their control. In recent years, tyranny of Bhojpur landlords had been on the increase. For example, in 1972 atrocities on Harijans numbered 98; in 1973–109; in 1974–259; in 1975–300; in 1976—1130. In 1977 on 11th March, the entire village–Bhumihartola was burnt to ashes, old and women were killed indiscriminately. The aggravation of tyranny was caused by the organised resistance of the Harijans. Heroic resistance of Harijans is exemplified in death-defying stand of their leader–Butan Mushahar. With the gun of the enemy aimed at him, he thundered—"I am Butan Mushahar, the Commander of the Red Army of Bhojpur; what else you want to know?'l Tearing his shirt to expose the chest he said: "If you want to know more, shoot me here. Then only you will know the aguish of my heart". Bonded labourer Ganesh Doshad not only annihilated class enemies: he-also established a sort of revolutionary government: land of Zamindars was confiscated, grain from their godowns was distributed and confiscated lands were collectively cultivated. The State power demolished that government. However, the 'banihar' system has been abolished from the area.

The problem in our villages is abject submission of the Harijans and low caste Hindus to the domination by upper caste land owners and moneylenders. Non-resistance against tyranny is an incentive for the tyrant to persist in his heinous atrocities. Active resistance on the part of the oppressed does risk increased tyranny but in the end the victory of the people's war is inevitable.

TABLE I

Statistics of crimes against Scheduled Castes under IPC during 1982, 1983 and 1984.

State/U.T.	Murder			Grievous Hurt			Rape		
	1982	*1883*	*1984*	*1982*	*1983*	*1984*	*1982*	*1983*	*1984*
1. Andhra Pradesh	16	11	17	08	26	08	17	25	15
2. Bihar	72	71	95	205	152	179	97	87	83
3. Gujarat	13	20	13	66	48	63	06	08	10
4. Haryana	01	01	03	21	01	03	59	23	26
5. Himachal Pradesh	01	02	Nil	02	04	07	02	03	04
6. Jammu and Kashmir	02	01	—	02	01	—	05	02	01
7. Karnataka	19	15	16	05	05	02	06	09	13
8. Kerala	04	07	08	05	01	06	07	18	08
9. Madhya Pradesh	88	108	122	366	323	351	148	183	213
10. Maharastra	19	17	10	85	73	31	48	35	39
11. Orissa	10	09	08	16	16	13	11	07	09

12.	Punjab	13	08	06	08	09	03	08	07	10
13.	Rajasthan	57	35	24	174	174	192	58	75	63
14.	Tamilnadu	05	14	06	05	07	15	02	08	17
15.	Uttar Pradesh	208	202	213	457	507	580	152	148	176
16.	West Bengal	06	04	–	02	04	04	04	01	04
Union Territories										
1.	Delhi	–	–	–	–	–	–	01	–	–

Vide Committee on the Welfare of Scheduled Castes and Scheduled Tribes (1985-86) 11th Report 8th Lok Sabha.

TABLE 2

Government Executives as on 1.7.1984 in districts identified as sensitive from the point of view of crimes against SC/ST

Name of State	*Dist. Magistrate*			*Supdt. of Police*			*Sub divisional Magistrote*			*Subdivisional PO*		
	Total	SC	ST	Total	SC	ST	Total	SC	ST	*Total*	*SC*	*ST*
1. Bihar	38	6	2	40	6	6	82	1	3	78	4	4
2. Madhya Pradessh	45	8	4	45	7	3	155	15	16	64	3	8
3. Rajasthan	27	4	–	27	2	4	84	10	4	123	7	5
4. Tamilnadu	16	2	–	60	10	2	54	4	–	249	13	2
5. Uttar Pradesh	57	10	2	80	11	–	361	53	5	241	24	–

9

Caste and Slavery

Slavery was abolished in Travancore State in 1855 but it persisted in veiled form of attached labour system. However, the soil serfs could not be sold as before. Both Pulayas and Parayas constituted agrestic slave castes in Kerala, particularly in Kuttanand area. During 19th century the tenancy reform increasingly conferred ownership rights on the 'tenants' and this led to a decline in landless transactions which in turn resulted in the decline in the practice of slaves changing hands. The slaves were retained by the persons who began to enjoy permanent ownership right on land and this led to the emergence of the *system of attached labour*.

Following the Slavery Abolition Proclamation, slaves were legally free and the sale of slaves was prohibited. The slave-owners skillfully gave up the practice of sale and mortgage of slaves. The attached labour system had all the characteristics of slavery, except that the attached labourer could not be transferred. In the absence of any State measure to provide economic sustenance, the freed slaves were compelled to remain dependent on their masters or owners. The structural features of caste also played a role in the transition from slavery to attached labour. The form of slavery in our country is intimately connected with the caste system. All types of servile status had been hereditary and the serfs or slaves all belonged to low castes/ Untouchables. Pulayas in Malabar are known as "Churnar" which is the corrupted from of Chammar (slave).

Pulays and Paragas are the lowest castes in Kerala, who were slaves and later transformed into attached labourer. They were not allowed to own or lease land and so they could not become 'tenants'. The ban relegated them to the level of landless agricultural labourers. Moreover, the laws of pollution prevented the Pulayas, Parayas and other slave castes from entering into any craft or trades which required intercourse with upper castes. The laws of pollution pushed them to wetland cultivation, which is very unhealthy, untidy and a hard type of labour. The slave castes were not allowed to work in the drylands which were adjoining the houses of upper caste land owners and tenant cultivators.

Kuttanad area with its geographical and climatic constraints has the labour intensive conditions of 'punja' cultivation and the land owner employ the slave castes as attached labour. Land in Kuttanand is mainly held by the Brahman families known as 'Brahma-Swami' The temple authorities called 'Devaswami' constituted of Brahmans and few Nair Chieftains. The tenants who leased land from Brahmans and Nairs belonged mostly to the Nair and Syrian Christian communities. It is notable that the Ezhavas who occupied a status intermediate between Nairs and Pulayas are not banned from leasing land. However, they get only small parcels of land on sub-lease basis from Nair or Syrian Christian tenants.

It is heartening to note that as a result of struggles of attached labourers, *the system of the veiled slavery collapsed in 1943* and the collection of clay became a more paying occupation than ordinary agricultural labour. But few Ezhava were in this occupation. Collection of clay still remains a Pulaya and Paraya activity.

The collapse of the attached labour system was not a mechanistic outcome of the development of capitalist investment in punja cultivation. The credit goes to the activities of Communist Party of Travancore. The success of the strike at Keralem in raising the quantity of paddy from 25 paras to 75 paras as 'Adayam' inspired the labourers in other parts of Kuttanad. Since then the farmers owning land could no longer enforce continued attachment by creating indebtedness through manipulation of work accounts. They, therefore, began to reduce the number of attached labourers under them. It was the labour movement which contributed significantly to its disintegration. Thus *slavery of the low caste population could be ended through organised class struggle.*

Under 1976 Bonded Labourer System (Abolition} Act, all bonded labourers were declared free, discharged from the obligations and had their debt liquidated. The State Governments have reported that upto March 31, 1987 some 209, 285 bonded labourers have been identified and freed, of whom 185, 083 had been rehabilitated. But *the Bonded Liberation Front says a conservative estimate of the number of labourers still bonded is 5 million of whom 80-90 percent belong to Scheduled Castes and Scheduled Tribes* (Economic Times 6.8.89).

According to one national level survey undertaken during the year 1978, it had been estimated that *66% of the identified bonded labourers belonged to Scheduled Castes and 18% to the Scheduled Tribes.*

The Committee on the Welfare of Scheduled Castes and Scheduled Tribes (1985-86) with Shri Krishan Datt Sultanpuri as the Chairman noted: "Inspite of various legislative and administrative measures taken and protective legislations enacted by the State Governments/Union Territory Administrations the exploitation of the poor Scheduled Castes/Scheduled Tribes still continues unabated. This is evident from the fact that the bonded labour system is still prevalent in many States; land belonging to Scheduled Castes/Scheduled Tribes is being alienatted and they are also denied the statutory minimum wages". The Committee members were mostly from the ruling Congress Party—so there is least likelihood of any exaggeration. The Committee itself commented: "There are no precise estimate as to how many bonded labourers are there in the country". Estimates of 3 organisations—State Government, NSSO and Gandhi Peace Foundation are 120561, 345000 and 2617000 respectively!

TABLE 1

The number of landed agricultural labourers (in thousands) according to 1971 census

—Bonded Labourers—

State	*Estimate of State Govt.*	*NSSO*	*Gandhi Peace Foundation Jan., 1981*
Andhra Pradesh	12,701	7300	3,25,000
Assam	—	4400	—
Bihar	4218	102400	1,11,000
Gujrat	42	4200	17,100
Haryana	—	12,900	—
Himachal Pradesh	—	—	—
Jammu and Kashmir	—	900	—
Karnataka	62,689	14,100	1,93,000
Kerala	700	400	-
Madhya Pradesh	1531	1,16,200	5,00,000
Maharastra	—	4,300	1,00,000

Continued

Manipur	—	—	—
Meghalaya	—	—	—
Nagaland	—	—	—
Orissa	337	5,400	3,50.000
Punjab	—	4,300	—
Rajasthan	6,000	2,400	67,000
Tamilnadu	27,874	12,500	2,50,000
U.P.	4469	31,700	5,50,000
W. Bengal	—	21,600	—
All India	1,20,561	3,45,000	26,17,000

TABLE 2

The number of landless agricultural labourers (in thousands) according to 1971 census

	Total labourers	*Peasants*	*Landless agricultural labourers*	*Other labourers*
India	180373	78177	47489	54707
		(43.34)	(26.34)	(30.32)
Andhra	18006	5795	6829	5382
Pradesh		(32.18)	(37.93)	(29.89)
Assam	4240	2410	406	1424
		(56.84)	(9.58)	(33.58)
Bihar	17489	7580	6806	3103
		(43.34)	(38.92)	(17.74)
Gujarat	8395	3620	1888	2887
		(43.12)	(22.49)	(34.39)

Continued

Haryana	2654	1303	431	920
		(49.10)	(16.24)	(34.66)
Himachal Pradesh	1278	903	53	322
		(70.66)	(4.15)	(25.19)
Jammu and Kashmir	1374	890	42	442
		(64.77)	(3.06)	(32.17)
Kerala	6216	1107	1908	3201
		(17.81)	(30.69)	(51.50)
Madhya Pradesh	15296	8085	4062	3149
		(52.86)	(26.56)	(20.58)
Maharastra	18390	6537	5394	6459
		(35.55)	(29.33)	(35.12)
Manipur	371	248	13	110
		(66.85)	(3.50)	(29.65)
Meghalaya	447	309	44	94
		(69.13)	(9.84)	(21.03)
Mysore	10179	4073	2718	3386
		(40.01)	(26.71)	(33.28)
Nagaland	262	203	4	55
		(77.48)	(1.53)	(20 99)
Orissa	6851	3368	1937	1546
		(49.16)	(28.27)	(22.57)
Punjab	3913	1665	787	1461
		(42.55)	(20.11)	(37.34)
Rajasthan	8049	5226	749	2074

Continued

		(64.93)	(9.31)	(25.76)
Tamilnadu	19742	4608	4490	5644
		(31.26)	(30.46)	(38.28)
Tripura	432	235	86	111
		(54.80)	(19.91)	(25.69)
Uttar Pradesh	27334	15698	5454	6182
		(57.43)	(19.95)	(22.62)
West Bengal	12369	3955	3272	5142
		(31.97)	(26.46)	(41.57)

N.B: Figures within bracket represent percentages.

The above table indicates that the states of Bihar, Andhra Pradesh, Tamilnadu and Kerala have 30% or more landless agricultural labourers. The problem of *caste-atrocity* is also more acute in these states. According to 1661 census. 72.6% of the total population of our country are engaged in agriculture and they are either SC/ST or OBC.

10

Caste and Politics

Politicization of caste is a by-product of the general process of social and political changes that started following the imposition of British rule in 18th century. The introduction of English education, the growth of modern professions, the emergence of the new middle class, the expansion of the market economy and the gradual extension of franchise (beginning with the Act of 1861) and cultiminating with the introduction of universal adult franchise slowly but surely affected the traditional caste system.

The upper castes already enjoying an upper social status took to Engltsh education and modern professions and thereby added still another element of high social status to their armoury. The lower castes, on the otherhand, first sought upward social status by demanding to be recorded in the Census (first started in 1867-71) as belonging to higher 'Varna' than previously accorded to them and by 'Sanskritising' their ritual and life-style to bring them closer to upper castes. But such caste mobility was not always successful and proved to be impossible for the Untouchables. Moreover, the British Government discontinued the practice of recording caste figures in the Census (after 1931). The people belonging to Scheduled Caste and Scheduled Tribe particularly those in urban areas with some degree of academic qualifications have developed a vested interest in continuing to be listed as scheduled caste or scheduled tribe. The result is that 'Sanskritization' has been supplanted by 'Westernization' i.e. acquiring education, joining modern profession and entering politics. And caste and to an extent, tribe also became available as basis for the political mobilization. Caste-based organisations are, now-a-days quite active in cities and towns.

Scheduled Caste and Scheduled Tribe people are more or less uniformly backward and poor, whereas the 'other backward class/caste' people are an extremely heterogeneous category including at one end, the rich, powerful and socially high status members of the dominant landowning caste and very poor members of the artisans, and labouring class at the other. Thus in the case of the category of OBC, caste and class would seem to converge, on the other hand, the term 'Other Backward Class', given currency through government publications, is a misnomer, because one's economic status is not the determining factor in one's membership of this category. However, the *Mandal Commission applied social, educational and economic criteria to determine the membership of OBC*. The central government has not yet accepted recommendations of the Mandal Commission and recognise only the landless agricultural labourers as OBC. The 'other backward classes' were originally listed for a scheme of preferential treatment. However, things have changed because several State Governments came gradually to be dominated by dominant land-owning middle peasant class. Their political leaders exploiting the legislative majority legislated in favour of their castes the same provisions of protective discrimination as those extended to SC and ST population. Karnataka reserved a total of 58% of jobs for OBCs. But in Maharasthra, the Marathwada University is yet to be named Ambedkar University.

The scheme of protective discrimination was adopted as a measure to enable the backward castes/classes to catch up with the more advanced sections i.e. the upper castes. The idea was to disengage the convergence between caste and class. However, it is well known that its benefits have been largely taken away by a few influential and relatively advanced individuals and families of SC and ST. The fact is that every subcaste and group at every level of the hierarchy has few kin groups or sections which are better off and politically more influential and they tend to monopolise the benefits allotted to the caste as a whole, denying them to those in far greater need. This is a sort of piggy-back system, a few riding on the backs of many, and this occurs all along the line. The low castes seem to have learnt it from the high castes.

Currently, caste identities take on new forms of articulation, thus changing the very ethics of the social system and diminishing the importance of its ritualistic basis and more diverse forms of organisations and interest identification enter the political system thereby giving rise to highly mobile, cross-cutting loyalty structure in parliamentary politics. Thus electoral politics leads both to the federation as well as fragmentation of castes in common organisations.

Politicisation of caste is in a way a step towards progress. 'It is not politics that gets caste-ridden, it is caste that gets politicised'. Politicisation of caste results in outwardlooking, upwardmoving orientations and this leads to secular outlook. The operation of competitive politics has drawn caste out of its political context and given it a new status that the 'caste system' as hitherto known has got eroded and has begun to disintegrate.

Casteism in politics is nothing but politicisation of caste. In this process both caste and politics are brought nearer. In caste, politics finds material for its articulation and mould it into its own design. In making politics the sphere of activity, caste groups get an opportunity to assert their identity and to strive for social position and political power. Politicians find in caste, an extremely well articulated and flexible basis for organisation.

While the caste associations function for a cause which is primarily social, they prepare the background for the transformation of social identity into political identity. Had other avenues of social advancement and status improvement been available to the aspirant caste groups, it is doubtful whether politics would have been so much influenced by caste as it is. Owing to the extremely under-developed nature of social mobility, politics, when it assumed some importance in acquiring power and prestige, increasingly came to be pressed into service to function as vehicle for social and political aspiration.

The caste-based society provided a cultural base for a common Indian identity but India rarely had a unified State structuse. This is particularly so with regard to South India, which was rarely directly snbject to powers that ruled the Gangetic plain. The Gangetic plain, on the other hand, was more often under the rule of a single kingdom. During 1857 uprising, the men of money were all on the side of British whereas some of the feudals joined the peasants and the rebel soldiers in fighting the British rule. In those days, Lala Jyotiprasad, Nansilal Abechand and Muttra Sethjis financed the British authorities. The merchants in general allied themselves to the power that seemed likely to win and to be able to provide the settled conditions necessary for trade and banking.

Indian merchant communities are of two kinds: those involved in long distance trade and finance (banking) activities; and those who were peddlers and retailers. Profits in trade and finance were made mainly by the former and the accumulation thereof could scrvc as the basis for a transition to industry. In ritual terms in the caste hierarchy, these long distance merchants and bankers had a higher status. They, like the Marwari and Gujarati Banias and the Aggarwal and Vaish communities of U.P were recognised as Vaishyas—the dwijas (twice born). Nattukotai Chettiars were the exceptions. The other kind of merchants i e. the retailers and peddlers were mostly of Shudra caste e.g. the Sahas and Tilis of Bengal. In Punjab, the ascending scale of caste status distinguished the banking and merchant communities from peddlers, carriers, cattle dealers, grain-grocers and liquor and meat sellers.

It is noteworthy that the practices of merchant bankers were influenced by caste consideration; they favoured their caste fellows and discriminated against outsiders. Credit and trade terms were easier for those of Bania caste; Marwaris who controlled Calcutta's banking system favoured their caste fellows and did not put their money in bank stocks where it could serve the general trading interest.

The first to make the transition from trade to industry were the merchants of Bombay, like the Jeejibhoys and Tatas. The Banias of Gujarat, like the former, imported British manufactures and exported Indian cotton. They all had interests in shipping and the China trade. The Marwaris acted as merchants, moneylenders and bankers in the interior of the country and they rather rarely acted as middleman of foreign economic interest. They were important both in the internal trade of the country and in procuring raw materials for export, though not in the actual export. They included the Birlas, Singhanias and Thapars. The third group came from among the moneylending landowners like Goenka and Bangur. Thus it was those who were most intimately connected with the colonial and feudal exploitation of the country that made the transition to capitalist industry.

For the big bourgeoisie, nation building became a matter of fashioning in India on the basis of a Hindu/Hindi ethos. The Hindi heartland is the Hindu heartland as well, where the caste satisfaction is found in its classical elaboration. In Uttar Pradesh, Rajasthan, Madhya Pradesh and Bihar, Rajputs and Banias existed in close juxtaposition, one representing the Kshatriya varna and the other the Vaishya varna; both belonging to the Dwija status. Beyond this Hindi heartland, the varna order tend to be imperfectly articulated—with Brahmans and Shudras preponderating at the two poles. Indian national movement dominated by big bourgeois interest adopted the policy of pan-Indian nation and non-Hindi big bourgeois groups, such as Gujarati Banias as well as some upper caste groups which were not big bourgeoisie, interested in all-India markets like the Tamil Brahmans supported Hindi as national language. *Hindu/Hindi ethos is a kind of upper caste Hindu ethos.* It is due to influence of this section, idea of forced union in a centralised state is favoured against a willing federation.

The pan-Indian big bourgeoisie represented by the Indian National Congress preferred partition of India to a federation. The federation would not have only helped the growth, not of just Muslim bourgeoisie but also other competing regional bourgeoisie. Birla, in particular, explicitly went in favour of partition. Thus Indian big bourgeoisie laid the basis for building the State with the addition of an upper caste Hindu/Hindi ethos.

Motivation for politicisation of religion comes less from religious fanaticism and more from political ambitions; loyalty to the religious prejudice of caste is utilized for this purpose. The middle class Hindus belonging to upper and intermediate castes who have acquired economic clout are getting more and more communalised. Religion is also utilized by those who are getting increasingly sidelined in politics. For example, the Brahmans who are losing their monopoly in political power, are floating religio-political organisations to reassert their political presence. Caste-based political organisations are thus confined to not only Untouchables or tribals. The influence of caste is so pervasive that the secular communist party in Andhra Pradesh became dominated by the caste of Kamma who are mostly landowners. It is said that even the heroic Telengana struggle did not go against the interest of these Kammas!

About the caste composition of the 'left' political parties of West Bengal, Ashok Mitra (Calcutta Diary, p. 66) remarked:

"There may be thitty incarnations of leftism in West Bengal. None can thrive without being shepherded by upper caste Hindu ministrels. Now and then, an occasional aberration, the section of the working class family has come to the fore, but by and large, *the roster of names stradling the entire spectrum of the left leadership follows a set pattern. Begin with Das Guptas and Lahiris and end with the Majumdars and Chatterjees, all impeccable high caste names, either Brahman or Vaidya or Kayastha*". In fact, the leaders of almost all the All India political parties are from the upper caste Hindu gentry with feudal heritage, upbringing and outlook.

With regard to the leadership of the communist dominated Kisan Sabha, in Bihar, Walter Hauser, the charitable biographer of Swami Sahajanand Saraswati wrote: "Socially the Kisan Sabha leadership was predominantly Bhumihar and there were also Rajputs, Brahmans and Kayasthas, but in very small numbers; variation in the social composition of leadership appeared at the district level where locally prominent castes were found, with occasional Kurmis and Keoris. The Bhumihar dominance simply neglected the strength of that group as the major element among the 'landed gentry' and 'adventurers' in the period. In terms of class background, *the Kisan leaders were primarily from landholding families*, in some areas of considerable means, more generally of moderate holdings, and in few cases from small-holding families". Caste and class pulls on them was obvious. Even Swami Sahajanand Saraswati in his early political career, as a resident of a subsidised Ashram at Bihta taught the Bhumihar landlords the virtues of 'purohitai'!

In Bihar, the Gopi Jatiya Sabha was formed in 1912 and was spread to all cow-herding castes extending from Punjab to Bengal. The Ahir movement had a monthly journal 'Ahir Samachar'. To this organisation even the Kurmis joined. Kurmis, however, had their own organisation–*Kurmi Mahasabha.* During thirties the three backward castes grew closer – Ahirs, Kurmis and Koeris joined together, and formed *'Triveni Sangh' in 1934*. Its membership was 1,000,000. The Congress leader Anugraha Narayan Sinha (Mere Sansmaran. p. 4) remarked: "... over the last 15 years that as long as the Congress kept its members away from the clutches of governmental institutions and posts of an enslaved India, the evil of casteism was avoided in Bihar but *as soon as the Congress members became entrenched in power, casteism spread* ... "

The leaders of Triveni Sangh (which had Harijans and Muslims also as its members) being educated and economically landowners could not espouse the cause of poor peasants and agricultural labourers and consequently in the eyes of other backward-caste sections, the organisation came to be viewed solely as an Ahir Kurmi–Koeri syndicate. The caste response to an essentially class problem–'abwabs', 'begar', 'bakast' failed to eliminate the influence of Congress which protected the interests of landowning class.

However, in Bihar tyranny of upper caste landowners are no longer viewed by educated backward boys as in the past (Servility of their forefathers). There are different views. Pranav Chatterjee (SSP) alleged that caste arrogance continued-Doms (sweepers) are mercilessly assaulted by the upper castes as well as the Police. Kesari Master: "Nothing had basically changed. Except that some of us got surnames like 'Singh' and the sacred thread. There is no 'begar' but *our women are still raped*. The dignity that the Sangh had created still moved us when we saw atrocities continue. Without us the Naxalite movement could not have taken place". (Bhojpur, Naxalism in the Plains of Bihar, p. 40).

There is no doubt that politicization of caste has resulted in political consciousness among the backward castes and Untouchables. Educational backwardness among them is primarily responsible for adherence to traditional beliefs and customs which act as the principal obstacle to class consciousness. Caste organisations are getting more and more politicalised but there is hardly any development of class consciousness. In the ninth Lok Sabha election, the opposition to Congress (I) has emerged with a fairly stable caste coalition popularly known as AJGAR (Ahimr, Jat, Gujjar and Rajput).

Dalits:

Since the middle of seventies, the politics of Dalits or 'depressed' has assumed importance and gained recognition by other political organisations. The word 'Dalit' is used in the political terminology since the formation of. *Dalit Panther' in Maharashtra*. Even though Dalit Panther could not achieve an all-India status and remained mostly restricted to Western India the voice of Dalits is now-a-days heard in other parts of the country. In Punjab assembly election, an organisation of Dalits could ensure the defeat of Congress (I), though it lost to Akali Dal. However, it is notable that dalit politics does not have much impact in the Eastern and Southern parts of India. In the three States of West Bengal, Kerala and Tripura where CPI (M) is strong, caste based dalit movement could not get a foothold!

Who are the dalits? In 1981 census, out of 75 crores of total population, 35 crores had been below poverty line. *Dalits are those Indians below the poverty line who are outcastes or Untouchables.* The word 'Harijan' was used by Gandhiji, and according to Government documents they belong to group titled as 'Scheduled Caste' and 'Scheduled Tribe'. Dalit movement remains weak for the simple reason that it excludes many genuinely depressed and includes a good number of low caste Hindu exploiters.

In Indian politics, no serious attempt has ever been made by any political party for the solution of caste inequality. During thirties when peasants were being mobilised and organised within All-Indian Kisan Sabha, Swami Sahajananda failed to realise the importance of caste stratification as a hindrance to class unity. *The AIKS did not pass a resolution on untouchability till 1945 and never considered cultural level struggles of importance.* The same is true for CPI. The book 'Marxist Cultural Movement in India' does not contain the word castes! Paradoxically, 'The Platform of Action of the CPI, 1930' stated: "The Communist Party of India fights for the complete abolition of slavery, the caste system and the caste inequality in all its forms (social, cultural etc.)". B.T. Ranadive claimed that communist party was the only party which linked the struggle against untouchability and caste system with agrarian revolution! The reality is that the communist party never had a programme regarding caste inequality and oppression, it only had a subjective formulation on caste!

In recent years, there has been a transformation of the downtrodden Untouchables/low caste Hindus from the passive human mass into a socially conscious fighting class. This has been possible for the following three developments:

(1) Accentuation of poverty as a result of the growth of market economy and capitalist development. Poor has become poorer and rich richer.

(2) Emergence of a critical consciousness among the poor as a result of decline of fatalistic outlook.

(3) Emergence of radicals in the political field as the revolutionaries of a new outlook on poverty linking with exploitation by exploiters.

However, the influence of caste system on Hindu elites has been described by R.P. Dutt as 'the disastrous "combination of political radicalism and social reaction in India".

Attitude of dalits towards socialist revolution is expressed in Dr. Ambedkar's writing (The Annihitation of Caste): "Men will not join revolution for the equalisation of property unless they know that after the revolution is achieved they will be treated equally and that there will be no discrimination of caste and creed. The assurance of the socialist leading the revolution that he does not believe in caste, I am sure, will not suffice." We must recognise that from the ranks of dalit/caste organisation of non-Brahmans has arisen rationalist movement in our country. Most of the present day caste-based organisations have put themselves outside the pale of the growing left and democratic movement. It is the duty of the revolutionary radicals to wean the honest elements from dalit/caste organisation to engage them in the task of building class unity amongst the downtrodden masses.

An Untouchable wishes to be called 'dalit' (what he really is) instead of the euphemistic name given by Gandhiji. His ideas about the policy of the government is succinctly reflected in his statement: "Don't you know if the 10-year reservation is ended and the inducements that keep the dalits within the Hindu fold are no more, leading political parties (including the ruling party) would be found grovelling in dust". He thus threatened the possibility of 370 million SC/ST may make common cause with more than 100 mlllion Muslims.

Dalits, now-a-days boast that the two great Indian epics and the Constitution were composed by them. A 'Bhangi' wrote the Ramayana, a 'Chamar' the Mahabharata and a 'Mahar' the Indian Constitution! Most of the upper caste Hindu intelligentsia tend to believe that SC/ST people are of low calibre and attribute the SC/STs presence in their midst as colleagues or seniors as a gift of reservation but it is not always so.

Recently Harijan in Bodinayakanur and its surrounding areas of Madura District of Tamilnadu, heavily out-numbered by Thevars and other upper caste Hindus are threatening to embrace Islam. The caste war is an outcome of political rivalry.

Caste System and thc Tribals:

Hindu caste system is so powerful and all-pervading that few tribes could escape its influence and consequences. In dealing with Hindus, the tribals fall under the influence of caste system because the Hindus judged and classed them according to their own standards. Hindus accorded the tribal that rank in their society which, in their opinion, the tribal deserves as judged by the tribals' habits regarding food and behaviour. Tribes that eat beef and the flesh of either 'unclean animals' or carry on profession which is unclean ritually, are regarded as impure and their touch is polluting. Many nomadic tribes fall under this category. Their professions include domestic service, broom making, playing musical instruments, public singing, dancing etc.

The majority of tribes have always aspired after Kshatriya rank and in particular claimed incorporation in the Rajput community. The claim is on the assumption of being descendants of Rajput ancestors. In fact, many Rajputs have intermarried with the upper strata of tribal community. For example, Rani Durgavati, mother of last Gond King of Mandla was a Rajput princess of Mahoba. It is also a historical fact that Rajputs married into the chief families of Korku and Bhil tribes.

In order to maintain a respectable caste status, some tribes refuse to accept food from any low caste member though originally such a discrimination was foreign to them. Thus Khandesh Bhils do not eat food cooked by Mahars, Mangs and Chamars. Gonds do not eat food cooked by Baigas, Balatis, Pardhans etc. Certain tribes refuse to accept food from any outsider, even when he is a Brahman!

There is a distinction between Hinduised section and a tribal section. The former generally consider themselves superior and refuse to interdine and intermarry with the tribal one. At the most, the Hinduised section takes wives from the tribal sections but refuses to give its daughter in marriage with the son of the latter.

The Hinduised tribals behave as upper caste Hindus towards the tribals who eat beef. They also regard tribes as inferior who serve them and accept food from them.

Tribes designated as 'Scheduled' were listed in a Presidential Order of 1950, which was modified in 1956. The *Scheduled Tribes consist of about 350 tribes*, each with its own distinct language, culture and social tradition. About 74 primitive tribes have been identified in 15 States and Union Territories and they constitute a priority group within Scheduled Tribes.

There had been formal mass conversions of tribals to Hinduism. For example, in the 18th century, Manipuris, Koches and Kachharis were declared Hindus of Kshatriya status. Brahmans also bestowed the sacred thread on large numbers of Raj Gonds of Mandla district in Gujarat. Vaishnavite Brahmans acted as missionaries and converted thousands of tribals to Hinduism. At the beginning of 19th century, *Swami Narayan converted many tribals to Hinduism.* Vishwanath (Brahman) converted 75,000 Bhils and Dhankas to Hinduism. Other Hindu monks, mainly Vaishnavas worked as missionaries among the Orans, Santals and 'Bhumij's.

However, conversion of tribals to Hinduism was rarely complete. Traditional beliefs and religious rituals were preserved by the tribals even after formal conversion.

TABLE 1

Tribal Population In India, According to 1971 Census

	(in lakhs)
Andhra Pradesh	16.50
Assam	19.20
Bihar	49.33

Gujarat	**37.34**
Madhya Pradesh	**83.87**
Maharastra	**29.54**
Manipur	3.34
Meghalaya	8.14
Karnataka	2.31
Nagaland	4.58
Orissa	**50.72**
Rajasthan	**31.26**
Tamilnadu	3.12
Tripura	4.81
U.P.	1.99
West Bengal	**25.33**
Arunachal Pradesh Union Territories	3.69

Total Tribal Population – 3,80,15,620=6.92% of Total Population.

In 1976, the total number of Tribals rose to 4.1 crores which was 7.5% of the total population.

Unlike the Untouchables or Scheduled Caste people, the *Adivasi or tribal population were not regarded as part of Hindu society till 1931* when, pressurised by the demands of Muslims for representation according to numerical strength, the upper caste Hindu leaders of the nationalist movement took the initiative of including them as Hindus in the Census Report. Compared to the SC people who meekly suffered without resistance, oppression by the upper class Hindus, the *Adivasis rose in revolt on repeated occasions against tyranny of foreign domination, landowners and money lenders.* Moral standard of an Adivasi is far superior to that of the upper caste Hindus including the Untouchables. *The yoke of caste system produced moral degradation of SC, not of ST.*

According to Act 342 of Indian Constitution, about 400 tribes or tribal communities have been included in the list of Scheduled Tribes. In West Bengal, the tribal population numbers 25,32,969 i.e. 6.66% of the total tribal population; of them 38 tribes belong to Scheduled Tribes.

Tribals of West Bengal can be divided into two groups:

(1) Those of plains—Santal, Munda, Oraon, Bhumija, Mahali, Kora, Lodha etc.

(2) Those of North Bengal—Bhutia, Lepcha, Chakma, Lerpa, Toto, Garo, Hajong, Mog, Mech, Mru, Rava etc. The former are governed by patriarchal ideology whereas the latter by matriarchal ideology. The former constitute 97% in number and their language is Dravidian in origin; the latter only 3% are Mongol in origin. *Tribes of Mongol origin are far ahead in education and employment in government jobs.*

TABLE 2

Scheduled Castes and Scheduled Tribes of West Bengal (1961 Census)

I.	Scheduled Tribes	Total 2,054,081 (5.88% of State's Total Population)
	Mainly made up of	
	Santals	Over 1,200.000
	Oraons	297,000
	Mundas	160,000
	Bhumijas	91,000
II.	Scheduled Castes	Total 6,890,314 (19.73% of State's Population)

Mainly made up of Rajabanshis	1,202,000
Bagdis	1,097,000
Pondhs	876,000
Nama-Sudras	727,000
Bowris	501,000

(Total of I and II =8,944,395 (25.61% of State's population). (From 'Bengal: The Communist Challenge' by Irani).

It is interesting to note that the Committee formed by the West Bengal Government in 1980 (August) opposed reservation of employment in Government services for Other Backward Classes and in the Parliament both Jyotirmoy Basu (CPM) and Geeta Mukherjee (CPI) stated that in West Bengal *there is no problem of social and educational backwardness related to caste system*! However, various organisations of backward classes complained to Mandal Commission that upper caste/minority Hindus are perpetuating domination over majority who are SC/ST or OBC.

11

Backwardness and Caste

The caste system is responsible for keeping the Hindu society divided in a hierarchial order and this has resulted in a close linkage between the caste rank of a person and his social, educational and economic status. The mode of stratifiction of the society provided the upper castes a deep-rooted vested interest in the perpetuation of the system. The priests (Brahmans by caste) held the lower castes in bondage for ages and this was done with full support of the ruling authority. The lower castes have always suffered from discrimination in all walks of life. Regarding relationship of poverty to social backwardness, the Supreme Court observed (in Balaji Case): "*Social backwardness is, in the ultimate analysis, the result of poverty to a very large extent.* These classes of citizens who are deplorably poor automatically become socially backward". However, it is also a fact that the lower and impure caste people had been permanently assigned menial task and refused any access to other avenue for a better life.

Criteria for Backwardness

Regarding the criteria of backwardness there had been a lot of controversy. Kaka Kalelkar, the Chairman of the First Backward

Classes Commission opposed the acceptance of caste as the basis backwardness. He argued: "the recognition of the specified castes backward may serve to maintain and even perpetuate the existing distinction on the basis of caste". He further added: "if the entire community, barring a few exceptions has thus to be regarded as backward, the really needy would be swamped by the multitude and hardly receive any special attention or adequate assistance nor could such dispensation fulfil the condition laid down in the Article 340 of the Constitution". Shri Kalelkar wanted to ignore the objective reality. In a particular low caste/subcaste, almost all the members are equally backward in their social, educational and economic status, so the question of multitude swamping the few does not arise at all. Report of the 'Research Planning Team of the Sociologists' after considering the context in which the provisions in the Constitution as well as the actual wording of the Conslitution, felt that these relate to socially recognising and persistent collectivities and not to individuals. The real reason behind Kalelkar's objection is revealed when he says: "If such communities have neglected education, it is because they had no use for it. *Now that they have discovered their mistake, it is for them to make the necessary efforts for making up the leeway*'. I am definitely against reservation in Government services for any community for the simple reason that services are not meant for the servants, but they are meant for the service of society as a whole". B.P. Mandal, the Chairman of the Second Backward Classes Commission aptly commented: "*The above extract form eloqueni testament of Shri Kalekar's views on backwardness and social justice. Such attitude towards the low caste Hindus on the part of highly placed upper caste Hindu celebrities is responsible for the hostiie attitude of caste-based organisations of low castes and Uotouchables.*" Shri Kalelkar's stand on caste system can not possibly be different from that of his mentor – M.K. Gandhi. The opposition to acceptance of caste as the principal, if not the only cause for social and educational backwardness is tentamount to ignoring the genesis of the evil. They were deprived of social and educational facilities. *It was not by choice that they remained backward.*

During the debate in the Parliament on the Amendment of Article 15 by the addition of Clause 4, Pandit Nehru observed: "We want to put on end to all those infinite divisions that have grown up in our social life. . We may call them by any name you like, the caste system of religious division etc." Whereas Dr. Amedkar the then Law Minister stated: "*What are called backward classes are. . nothing else but a collection of certain castes.*"

According to Mandal Commission, *nearly 78% of the respondents were of the view that caste should be accepted as a criterion for identifying backwardness.* Only 28% favoured acceptance of caste as the sole criterion. Most of the State Governments favoured caste as an important criteria for determining social and educational backwardness. Some States preferred economic criteria and some a combination of caste and economic status.

Regarding steps taken by the respective State Governments to remove disabilities, nearly 43 percent (Evidence by the Public) were of the view that no concrete steps had been taken so far. Nearly 82% of the respondents felt that OBC's i.e. Backward Classes other than SC and ST have to face a number of hurdles in securing employment or admission to institutions of higher education (Mandal Commission's Report).

The Mandal Commission concluded that "caste is an important factor in the identification of other Backward classes among Hindu communities. However, it must be remembered that *all kinds of backwardness on the part of low caste and scheduled caste Hindus are due* to *their economic backwardness*; and *caste factor played a great role in the perpetuation of economic backwardness.*"

Social backwardness refers to ascriptive status while educational backwardness refers to achieved status. The former undergoes hcange only over a length of time whereas faster change is possible in case of the latter. In the appraisal of social backwardness, we have to take into account two categories:

(1) Castes or ethnic groups which are traditionally assigned a low status;

(2) Traditional occupations which are assigned a low status but which are linked with specific castes or ethnic groups.

The low ritual caste status of an individual has a direct bearing on his social backwardness. *It is an imposition by the strong over the weak.* A low caste or scheduled caste Hindu is not himself responsible for his backwardness. *They were rendered backward by the socio-economic exploitive system.*

The low social status and filthy occupations were imposed on them; the right to live the life of a human being was denied to them.

The extreme inequality in the prevailing Hindu society is best manifested in the educational backwardness of Shudras and Untouchables. Till the introduction of resevation of seats for SC and ST candidates, nearly 90% of seats in medical and engineering colleges were filled by candidates from about 18 Per cent of higher castes. Regarding the status of Scheduled Caste and Scheduled Tribes in the field of higher education, Andre Beteille (Caste in Indian Politics) pointed out "*As Brahmins entered the institutions of higher learning, the professions and services, everywhere they formed cliques from which non-Brahmins were excluded.* Between 1892 and 1904, out of 16 successful candidates for ICS, 15 were Brahmins; in 1914,123 out of 128 permanent district Munshiffs were Brahmins; in 1944, 452 out of 650 registered graduates of the University were Brahmins".* *Over the period of 10 years from 1969 to 1978, only 10 candidates belonging*

*Quoted in G.V. Subbah Rao's 'Life and Times of K.V. Reddi, Rajamundry, 1957, p. 17-19.

to SC/ST got into IAS on the basis of merit. As late as 1976 and 1977, not a single SC/ST could make the grade in open competition. Similarly, only 6 SC/ST could get into IPS on the basis of merit during these 10 years.

After so much fanfare about literacy compagin, only 8.04% of ST females can read and write. Average literacy rate had been 5.3% in 1901, 16.1% in 1941, 16.4% in 1951 and 36.2% of the total population of the country in 1981.

According to 1981 census, SC and ST population were 15.75 and 7.76 percent respectively. With passage of time, they started moving to urban areas. At the time of 1961 census, out of the total SC population in the country, excluding Assam, *89.29% lived in villages.* The percentage went down slightly to 89.03% in 1971 and it further declined to 84.0% at the time of 1981 census. Similar trend is also observed in the case of ST population. While in 1961, 97.36% of the total ST population lived in villages or hamlets, their percentage declined marginally to 96.48% by 1971. During 1981 census, the percentage of ST population living in villages declined to 93.80%. Thus the number of SC/ST population in urban areas, at present would be nearly 16% and 6% of their total number. Thus *the problem of SC/ST literacy is mainly a rural problem.*

The condition of health care system in our rural areas is simply alarming; all the qualified medical practitioners are clustered in towns and cities and only quacks are to cater to the needs of rural population of whom overwhelming majority are SC/ST people.

The spread of education (literacy) is not uniform among the scheduled caste and scheduled tribe population. Hutton (Caste in India) provided the foll owing table indicating their population in literacy.

TABLE I

Caste and Agricultural Occupations in Bihar, 1951

	Brahmans	*Rajputs*	*Vaishyas*	*Backward Classes*	*SC & ST*	*Tribes and Abo-riginals*	*Others*
Nunber of families	491	429	372	3639	2210	207	2195
Percentage of total no. of families	5.1	4.5	3.9	38.1	23.2	2.2	23.0
Landowners	81 (71.84)	8.2 (8.32)	1.1 (0.72)	1.1 (7.22)	3.5 (13.90)	–	–
Tenants	—	78.6 (14.07)	31.7 (4.92)	44 (66.12)	15.4 (15.19)	–	–
Agriculture workers	—	6.3 (0.95)	18.0 (2.36)	35.2 (44.99)	66.6 (51.71)	–	–
Non-agricultural workers	19 (6.96)	6.9 (2.25)	49.5 13.68)	19.5 (53.60)	14.5 (24.01)	–	–
Total	100.0	100.0	100.0	99.8	100.0		

(Source : All India Agricultural Labour Inquiry, Rural Man Power and Occupational Structure, pp. 55-57).

N.B. : The figures in parenthesis indicate the dispensation of each occupational category over various castes.

TABLE 2

Position of Exterior (SC/ST) Castes in literacy (according to 1931 census).

Province of State	*Total Population*	*Total Hindu Population*	*Total Exterior Caste Population*	*Percentage of Exterior Castes on*		*Percentage of Exterior Castes who are literate*
				Hindu Population	*Total Population*	
India	350,529,557	237,195,140	50,195,770	21	14	1.9
Provinces	271.431,549	117,727,108	34,064,009	22	14	1.6
Bengal	50,114,002	21,570,407	6,899,809	32	14	5.0
Bombay	21,854,866	16,621,221	1,750,24	11	8	2.8
Madras	46,740,107	41,277,370	7,234,104	18	15	1.5
Delhi	636,246	399,863	72,883	18	11	1.4

From the above table, it is obvious that in 1931 even in Bengal where the city of Calcutta experienced the social reform movement initiated by Ram Mohan Roy, illiteracy among the Scheduled Caste and Scheduled Tribe population (exterior caste) was as high as 95%. Evidently *there was no impact of so-called "renaissance" on low caste people.* In Madras, Bombay and Delhi, illiteracy rate amongst them were 98.3, 97.2 and 98.6 respectively.

During 1961-1981, literacy rate increased by 12.28 percentage points for the total population of India, while among the SC and ST population, the increase was of the order of 11.27 and 7.36 percentage points respectively. The trend is slightly different among males and females. Among the males, literacy rate increased, the highest among SC males, by 14.85 percentage points, followed by non-SC/ST males (12.89 percentage points) and ST males (11.8 percentage points). Among the females, the trend is slightly different. The highest increase of 13.77 percentage point was registered by non-SC/ST females followed by SC females. The lowest increase was among ST females (5.15 percentage points).

Illiteracy rate is highest in Bihar, Jammu and Kashmir and Uttar Pradesh 73% to 74%. One-third of the households in our country do not have even one literate member. *More than 38% of the rural households do not have any literate member.* Among the four major cities, *Delhi has the highest percentage of households with no literate members (12.74%) while Calcutta, Bombay and Madras had 11.79%, 8.53%* and *6.90% respectively.*

TABLE 3

Scheduled Castes: Literates

	Males	*Females*	*Total*
India	16,168,575	5,524,733	22,393,308
Rural	12,658,891	3,601,484	16,260,375
Urban	4,209,684	1,923,249	6,132,933

(*Contd.*)

Scheduled Castes: Literacy Rates

India	31.12	10.93	21.38
Rural	27.91	8.45	18.45
Urban	47.54	24.34	36.60

Scheduled Castes: Total Population

India	54,210,594	50,544,329	1,04,754,623
Rural	45,354,781	42,642,211	87,996'992
Urban	8,855,813	7,901.898	16,757,631

In Bihar, the Kayasthas constitute the most literate caste. The Kayasthas are followed by Brahmans, Bhumihar Brahmans and the Rajputs. According to 1931 census the Kayasthas have been the most literate caste (372 per 1000) followed by the Brahmans (195 per 1000). The Bhumihars (136 per 1000) and the Rajputs (120 literatcs per 1000). Among the lower castes, for the Kurmis and Goalas there were only 40 to 50 literates per 1000 and the Telis had only 50 literate persons per thousands.

An analysis of admissions to B.A. classes in Patna college during 1936-1963 indicates that a large majority of students come from the four upper castes. Even among the upper castes, the prominence of the Kayasthas in education is remarkable. The Kayasthas as a caste use to utilise the educational facilities much more than others. It is notable that the number of Kayastha students has been decreasing over the years and this is true of upper castes in general. This decline in the number of upper caste students is contrasted with the slow but steady rise in the number of students from other castes. However, upper castes continue to dominate the field of education.

Role of Saints and Social Reformers:

Among the saints whose preachings contributed to the weakening of the rigidity of caste system, special mention is deserved by

Ramanand, Kabir, Chaitanya, Eknath, Tukaram and Ravidas. They all preached spiritual equality. However, they never condemned caste distinction observed by orthodox upper caste Hindus. As a result of their preaching, the toiling masses of the low castes had the opportunity, to an extent, of enjoying the right of participation in religious ceremonies.

Chaitanya did not openly try to do away with the caste system but he indirectly attempted to undo its evil effects. Bengal Vaishnavism did away with casteism to the extent that some of the non-Brahman followers of Chaitanya became acknowledged gurus who had Brahmans among their disciples. But this tendency of liberalism on question of caste propagated by Bengal Vaishanavs was checked by the Brindavan School! *Chaitanya himself, all through his life, acted according to Manu's directives on caste*. He never took cooked food from low caste people. Not only that, he never ate food in the house of a non-Brahman. He refused to accept alms from non-Brahmans. *His disciple Haridas was not allowed to enter into Hindu temples*! However, he did not hesitate to bury with his own hand the deadbody of Muslim Haridas.

Ramakrishna Paramhansa is famous for his liberalism but he *strictly observed all the rules and regulations of caste system*. He was very particular about food; not only he refrained from taking food cooked by non-Brahmans, he never liked to take food in the house of a non-Brahman. To Vivekananda, *he frankly admitted his adherence to the superstitution of caste*. According to him, caste division can be abolished only by 'bhakti'! Swami Vivekananda though a saint, had the vision to proclaim: "A time will come when the Shurdas of every country . . . will gain absolute supremacy in every society. The first glow of the dawn of this new power has already begun to slowly break upon the western world. Socialism, Anarchism, Nihilism and such other sects, are the vanguards of the social revolution that is to follow" (Caste, Culture and Socialism – pp. 79-80).

Apart from Ramakrishna Mission sponsored reform movement under his leadership, Brahmo Samaj (Ram Mohan Roy), Prarthana Samaj of Bombay and Arya Samaj of Dayanand Saraswati did commendable contribution to popularise the ideas of spiritual equality. However, *all these movements were confined to the middle class urban elites*, with absolutely no impact on the toiling masses of either urban or rural areas.

In Maharastra, during the second half of 19th century, the notable social reformers were M.G. Ranade, Dadoba and Jyotiba Phooley. It is *Jyotiba Phooley** with the support of Ranade, who opened primary schools for the Untouchables. Maharaja of Kohlapur also supported the adventure. In South India, Justice Party was organised mainly to fight for employments and higher education in favour of non-Brahmans. The movement was, later on, supported by 'Dravida Kadagam' led by E.V. Ramaswamy Periyar whose attacks against Tamil Brahmans, Hindi and North often overshadowed his other programmes of social reform such as eradication of superstitious practices and untouchability. The DK movement ultimately became DMK movement under the leadership of Annadurai, the beloved leader of southern people, Tamils in particular. Whatever improvement in the status of Untouchables in regard to emploment, education and political representation has been achieved, is mainly due to movement under the leadership of Dr. Ambedkar.

By the end of 19 th century, the issue of social reform receded into background and English educated intellengentsia turned their attention to obtaining more political concessions from the British rulers. Tilak, the then topmost leader of the Indian National Congress became the leader of anti-social reform group

*He is the pioneer in the anti-caste and social reform movement. People called him 'Mahatma'; his greatness is candidly depicted in Shyam Benegal's film "Bharat-Ek-Khoj". He wrote a book titled 'Golam-giri' portraying the horrible condition of Untouchables.

and Untouchables proved to be ephemeral after his death. The non-Brahman political party gradually dissociated itself from the movement for the emancipation of Untouchables, that was taking shape under the leadership of Ambedkar.

Gandhi's non-cooperation movement was an anathema to a large section of Brahman educated middle class of Maharastra. The non-Brahmans joined the Indian National Congress and the Brahmans left it (after Tilak's death) to join Hindu Mahasabha and the RSS was formed. After 1947, the intellectuals of the non-Brahman castes established a 'socialist party' titled '*Peasants and Workers' Party*. The INC in Maharashtra became mainly a party of Maratha peasantry united by strong caste bonds.

Unlike Marathas, there was no landed gentry nor any tradition of political power for the Untouchables. In medieval times, Mahars (Untouchables) were recruited to Maratha armies and this tradition continued upto the rule by the East India Company. In fact, the modern army gave the Mahars the opportunity to enter the modern age.

Lord Kitchener discontinued the recruitment of Mahars in the Army on the ground that Mahars do not belong to a martial race. The British rulers also wanted to cover up economic exploitation by the prevailing caste rules. *In 1891 he introduced the system of 'class company' in the army and divided the militaty into different caste groups and the Untouchables were thrown out.* The Mahars reacted by sending a memorandum and began a political movement for the emancipation of Untouchables. Organised struggle of Untouchables started in 1923 when Ambedkar returned from U.K. and U.S.A. and established 'Bahiskrita Hitakarini Sabha'. In the initial stage, the programme consisted of assertion of rights to public places and entry into temples. In 1927, a satyagraha was organised for drawing water from a public tank in Mehad (Colaba Distt) followed by satyagraha for temple entry in Pune and Nasik.

Role of Gandhi:

In the book "Romain Rolland and Mahatma Gandhi Correspondence" (Publication Division, Govt. of India) Gandhijis' position vis-a-vis Hinduism and caste system has been presented with eloquent clarity. Excerpts:

— Gandhi is religious by nature and his doctrine is essentially religious.

— Gandhi believes in the religion of his people, in Hinduism.

— In an article written on October 6,1925, Gandhi defines his conception of Hinduism (1) He believes, he says, in the Vedas, the Upanishads, the Puranas and all that goes by the name of Hindu seriptures. He believes therefore in Avatars and Rebirth. (2) *He believes in Varnasram Dharma or Disciplines of Caste*; in a sense which he considers strictly Vedic, but which may not correspond to the present popular and crude sense (3) He believes in the protection of cow in a much larger sense than the popular.

Rolland: I do not imagine that our present stage of development my explanation of Gandhi's views will make them seem acceptable as the caste system; nor am I anxious to have them seem so. I am inclined to think (he says) that the law of heredity is an eternal law and that any attempt to alter it must lead to utter confusion.

Gandhi: Varnasram or caste system, is inherent in human nature. Hinduism has simply reduced it to a science.

Gandhi believes in four classes or castes. The caste system, which deals with different classes of equal rank, bears no relation whatsoever to the attitude of Hindus to the untouchabies or pariahs.

Rolland: *Stay at home, shut all doors, change nothing, hold on to everything, export nothing, bury nothing, uplift and purify body and spirit. A gospel indeed, of medieval monks.* And

Gandhi, of the broad mind lets his name be associated with it.

"Gandhi says that he is a sanatani Hindu. And if Gandhi has finally fought against the crime of untouchability, *he has never sought to breach the caste system.* (This is another of the points for which Tagore finds it hard to forgive him). To Subhas Bose, Romain Rolland said about Gandhiji: "Gandhi enjoys great popularity in all parts and all classes of the country, but he is not using it to bring about effective action. No doubt he has done an immense amount over the last 15 years to revive the Indian national sentiment and *to bring the classcs together. But he is by nature a middle of the road man who is for ever seeking compromises between opposite extremes and parties. Thus he sincerely fights against untonchability but at the same time defends the caste system. Everywhere he is a restriction to progress.*"

Regarding Gandhjii's role, Dr. Ambedkar made a ruthless criticism exposing his role on the question of caste system and untouchability. Excerpts from his writings (Thus spoke Ambedkar Vol. II):

1. "Gandhi was a great protagonist of 'Chaturvarna and Varnashram' Dharma. *Whatever he did, it was not done for the emancipation of the Untouchables but for saving the Hinduism. His motive was political*". 2. The utterances like 'Two of my greatest desires that keep me in flesh and bone are the emancipation of Untouchables and the protection of the cow" and 'But if I have to be reborn, I should be born Untouchable' were mere platitudes meant for deluding the poor innocent Untouchables. Hindus, according to the Mahatma, are not sinful by nature'. Praising the most vicious and satanic social system of Hinduism popularly known as Varnashram which has disunited and ruined India, Gandhiji said to believe in Varnashram Dharma both according to birth and Karma. Further, he added "I do not want them (untouchables) to wrest their rights by violence as is done in the

west. 4. *I do not regard interdining and intermarriage as essentials to removal of untouchability*".

Gandhi: "But the reform contemplated in the untouchability movement does not obliterate the restrictions as the interdining and intermarriage. *I can not recommend the wholesale abolition of these rcstrictions to the public, even at the risk of being charged with hypocricy and inconsistency.* I can help you (Untouchable) in this (right to worship, education etc.) only following the way indicated by my religion and not by following western methods".

In my view, Gandhiji rather stood in the way of the Untouchables mobilizing themselves and played the role of a saviour and Avatar than arousing a revolutionary spirit against this savage system of ranking men by birth. N. Ram (Economic and Political Weekly, Annual number, 1979) rightly said: "E.V. Ramaswami's highly subjective alienation from the freedom movement on account of differences with the top congress leadership was provoked and fanned by a series of public positions adopted by Gandhi (especially during his visit to Madras) on social questions. Gandhi told a gathering in April, 1921 " . . . in Madras I have not a shadow of doubt that Hinduism owes its all the great traditions that the Brahmans have left for Hinduism . . . the Brahmans have declared themselves and *they ought to remain the custodians of the purity of our life*."

Dr. P.C. Joshi, at a conference on 'Planning of Social Change' said: "Perhaps Gandhi and his non-violence stood in the way of oppressed mobilizing themselves."

Gandhi (collected Works , Vol. 50, pp. 226-227) very clearly stated his views; "*Thc Varna system is ethical as will as economic. It recognises the influence of previous lives and heredity.* All are not born with equal powers and similar tendencies.

Neither the parents nor the State can measure the intelligence. But there would be no difficulty if each child is prepared for the professions indicated by heredity, environment and the *influence of former lives*; no time would be lost in fruitless experimentation, there would be no soul-killing competition, a spirit of contentment would pervade society and there would be no struggle for existence."

It is interesting to note that none of the 113 contributors to the volume (Mahatma Gandhi—edited by Radhakrishnan) make any mention of Gandhi's views or activities on the caste system.

Like Tilak, Gandhi also relied on revivalism. During the first non-cooperation movement he carried open campaign against everything Western including Western medicine, Western education and the railways. He harped on bringing back Ramraj. Critics have wrongly understood obscurantist outlook as the surrender to Hindu religious belief. *It was basically the surrender of the intelligentsia before the indigenous feudal system which sustained the caste system in Hindu society.* However, Gandhi did not hesitate to say: "If I seem to take part in politics, it is only because politics today encircles us like the coils of snake from which one can not get out, no matter how one tries. I wish to wrestle with snake. . *I am trying to introduce religion in politics.*"

When Rabindranath Tagore wrote: "An Appeal to Truth" as a cry of revolt against the blind obedience demanded by Nationalist leaders, Gandhiji's response was "*To renonunce tradition would be sinful.*" *He regarded the attempt at abolition of the tradition of caste system as sinful too.* And it was not sinful to practise 'Brahmacharya' at the age of 71 on unmarried young girls!

Role of Ambedkar:

Dr. Ambedkar's lifelong struggles against the caste oppression was constitutional on the one hand, and religious reforms on the other. Although initially he did organise a 'labour-Party' primarily with his caste (Mahar) followers and modelled on British Labour Party' and later on evinced interest in establishing certain sort of liaison with the Socialist Party led by Ram Manohar Lohia, *his out-look was basically rooted in the West Minister type of democracy, not in socialism.* He was a constitutional nationalist; his attitude toward British Government was best reflected in his address to the All India Depressed Classes Congress (1930): "I am afraid that the British chose to advocate unfortunate conditions not with the object of removing them but only because such a concern serves well as an excuse for retarding the political progress of India. So far as you are concerned, the British Government has accepted the arrangement as it found and has preserved them faithfully in the manner of the Chinese tailor who, when given an old coat as a pattern produced with pride an exact replica, rents, patches and all. Nobody can remove your grievances as well as you can and you can not remove them unless you get political power in your hands. No share of political power can come to you so long as the British Government remains as it is. It is only in a Swaraj constitution that you have chance of getting any political power into you own hands without which you cannot bring salvation to your people." His demand for land and separate colonies for Untouchables was justified because that is the way the Untouchables could escape serf dependence on other castes.

No one directed more concentrated fire against the Congress leaders and their hypocricy than Dr. Ambedkar.

Dalit movement under Ambedkar's leadership remained consistantly radical, on the land question. *It was Ambedkar who proposed a bill and led a march in 1936 for the abolition of 'Khoti' System in the Konkan area of Maharastra* aad attempted to arouse Mahars. Thus, Dalit movement initially had been a radical force for agrarian revolution and not just for the abolition of caste oppression. However, the All Indian Kishan Sabha—a mass organisation of CPI did not take any initiative to fraternise with the aspiration of Dalit peasants. Even though Dr. Ambedkar was an avowed anti-communist and a critic of Indian socialism he had an impressive programme on the land question. He said, "Neither consolidation (of land holdings) nor tenancy legislation can be of any help to 60 million Untouchables who are just landless labourers. *Only collective farms can help them.. Agriculture shall be a state industry.* Land will belong to the state and shall be let out to villagers, without distinction of caste or creed and in such a manner that there will be no landlord, no tenant, and no landless labourers."

It is a historical fact that the pressure from 'Dalit' workers acted as a counterweight to conservative and revivalist forces in the Indian National Congress to take a secular and 'democratic' stand.

It is significant that Dr. Ambedkar, the Chairman of the Drafting Committee of the Constitution remarked : .. We will have equality in politics and inequality in social and economic life. We must remove this contradiction at the earliest moment, *or else those who suffer from inequality will blow up the structure of political democracy.*"

Gandhiji stressed that conscience of upper caste Hindus had to be roused against the crime of untouchability whereas Dr. Ambedkar's emphasis was on evoking self-respect and the righteous anger of the Untouchables who had to rise and fight the atrocious Hindu caste system, an institution of social inequality imposed deliberately to maintain the system of exploitation. The difference between the two roles illustrates the failure of the forces of our freedom struggle. Gandhi could never rid his mind of a kind of fascionation for 'Varnasram' concept and he never asked people to give up caste system. Dr. Ambedkar was clear-cut in his view about caste system; he said: "The out-caste is a by-product of the caste system. *There will be outcastes as long as there are castes. And nothing can emancipate the outcaste except the destruction of the caste system.*" Gaadhiji argued that while "untouchability" was "the greatest blot on Hinduism" the whole system should not be pulled down and that "the excess" should first be "removed," but if the effort fails it will be time enough to consider how and by whom Varnasram is to be fought" (Quotations in D,G. Tendulkar, Mahatma, III, pp. 235).

Dr. Ambedkar was inflexible that untouchability must go lock, stock and barrel; and made a ruthless criticism of Brahmanism." "The religion which regards the recognition of man's self-respect as sin is not a religion but a sickness. The religion which allows one to touch a foul animal but not a man is not religion but a madness. The religion which says that one class may not acquire wealth, may not take up arms, is not a religion but a mockery of man's life. The religion which teaches that the unlearned should remain unlearned, that the poor should remain poor, is not a religion but punishment." Dr. Ambedkar had none of Gandhiji's Sanatanist qualm and Hindu caste system.

Gandhiji wanted to prune the tree by cutting down the unhealthy branches whereas Ambedkar demanded uprooting it.

CPI leader Hiren Mukherjee made an assessment of role of Gandhi and Ambedkar and commented. (Gandhi, Ambedkar and the extirpation of untouchability).

> "Mahatma Gandhi also can be faulted at many points in for far as his campaign against untouchability was concerned. There is no question about his passion, his moral, wholehearted detestation, but *his approach towards caste meant a halter round the neck of his principles.*"

> ". . , It is petty and hurlish to think of Ambedkar as pro-British and, therefore, suspect. Like almost all the galaxy of our 'social-reform' giants, he faces this charge which

> can be easily repelled. He was in the pursuit of a single, undeviating purpose, the upliftment of depressed classes which were borne of his bone and blood of his blood . . . In his own time and in face of grave obstacles, Ambedkar had played a patriotic, powerful and (in our im memorial and repeatedly unchanging Indian conditions) profound liberating role."

While Bankim Chandra Chattopadhyaya and Ramendra Sundar Trivedi castigated the role of Brahmans, Gandhiji extolled them!

12

Government Welfare Measures

At the Constituent Assembly (1946), Pandit Jawahar Lal Nehru sponsored a Resolutlon to the effect that measures for safeguarding the interests of backward classes of the Indian society would be introduced. The objective was made a part of the Indian Constitution. The safeguards in respect of Scheduled Castes and Scheduled Tribes included reservation of seats in the Parliament and State Assemblies, reservation of posts in services of the Central and State Governments and of seats in the institutions of higher education. Under a special provision of the Constitution, the office of the Commissioner for SC and ST was established in the 50's and as a supplement SC/ST Commission was instituted in 1978. The 1978 resolution was to be followed by a statute. But, as yet the Commission has not been given any Constitutional Status, not any powers under the Commission of Enquiry Act, as pleaded for by it in its successive reports. These constraints continue to detract from the effective functioning of the Commission. As a result most of the safeguards for SC and ST embodied in the Constitution continue to be violated with impunity and the guilty are scarcely booked.

Untouchability was outlawed in the Constitution of India. The document contains passages such as: "*Untouchabiliiy is abolished and practic in any from is forbidden* (Article 17) "all citizens shall have the right to practie any profession or to carry on any profession or to carry on any occupation, trade or business" (Article 19(g), and "no citizen shall be denied admission into any educational institution maintained by the State funds on grounds of religion, race, caste, language, or any of them" (Article 29(2).

Inspite of the careful definition of offences against SC/ST and the laying down of penalties for the wrong-doers, the law is generally observed in the breach. High caste police officials do not let themselves be shockeu or scandalised by gruesome atrocities against low castes. What then, SC/ST's ask, is the use of putting together yet another bill for the prevention of atrocities against SC/ST's and institution of special courts for expeditious disposal of police cases, if police keeps playing footsie with the violation of SC/ST's fundamental rights.

Prof. Nirmal Kumar Bose, a Gandhite was invited by the Government to join them as the Commissioner for Scheduled Castes and Scheduled Tribes. But, despite his membership of Indian National Congress, he did speak out the truth that, *under the garb of kindness to these castes and tribes, the Government was very often the worst enemy or that protecting their interests has become the portfolio of some self-seeking opportunists. And he could not survive the Government.*

Untouchability (Offences) Act, 1955 which was to deal with the cases of untouchability, did not prove effective enough. With effect from 19.11.1976, the name of the Untouchability (Offences) Act was changed to 'Protection of Civil Rights Act 1956' and some more stringent provisions were incorporated in the Act. The Committee on the welfare of SC and ST (1985-86) note that the practice of untouchability in some form or other is still prevalent in various parts of the country. A large section of SC are still illiterate and continue to live below the poverty line. Ii is a very distressing fact that there is only one voluntary Organisation of all-India nature namely, Harijan Sevak Sangh, Delhi which is engaged in the work of removal of untouchability.

The Annual Reports of SC/ST Commission have been emphasisting the importance of radical improvement in what are categorised as 'Unclean Occupations' especially scavenging and leather works, where untouchability is deeply entrenehed. The pursuit of modernization has not yet extended to these occupations. The abominable practice of night-soil being carried on head still persists in small towns. And there is no evidence of a scheme to improved condition of flayers and the method of flaying.

Studies conducted by SC/ST Commission found that only a few of the recipients (SC/ST) under the land reforms legislation, had been able to retain the assets for lack of wherewithals. The experience of bonded labourers, most of whom are SC or ST, is not different; vast numbers of Scheduled Caste people are engaged as agricultural labourers. The 'Minimum Wages' Acts enacted for their protection are in a similar state of implementation.

For the past decade, the SC/ST Commission has been stressing that it should be associated with planning and the Planning Commission should consult it with regard to strategies for development of SC and ST. But the Government have turned a deaf-ear towards what would appear as an eminently reasonable and constructive suggestion. Scheduled Caste Commission itself appears to be treated as untouchable!

There are a number of castes/subcastes which are treated as untouchable though they have not been included in the list of Scheduled Castes. Whereas some low caste people who are not untouchable are being included in the list of SC.

The State Governments which have launched programmes for the welfare of 'Other Backward Classes' have to fund the same from their own resources as no separate Plan allocation is made by the Centre for this purpose. According to Mandal Commission, other Backward Classes constitute only 12.55% of the total number of Government employees, whereas their aggregate population is 52%. Their representation in Class I jobs is only 4.69% i.e, less than 1/10th of their proportion to the total population. The Mandal Commission recommended: "Welfare programmes specially designed for OBCs should be financed by the Central Government in the same manner and to the same extent as done in the case of SC and ST." The Government of India have not accepted Mandal Commission's recommendation. It is heartening that the Commission forthrightly pointed out "Unless these production relations are radically altered through structural changes and progressive land reforms implemented rigorously all over the country, OBCs will never become independent."

Policy of Reservation

In a recently held seminar on 'Reservation Policy' Bhikha Bhai, Chairman of the National Commission for Scheduled Castes and Scheduled Tribes held that "Time is not yet ripe for discontinuing reservation". He argued that time has not yet come to substitute caste by class. *There is hardly any SC/ST candidate who has been able to be elected through the general constituency.* The policy of reservation of seats in Lok Sabha and State Assemblies by Articles 330 and 332 respectively has helped to improve the bargaining power of SC/ST in Lok-Sabha and State Assemblies but absence of reservation in Jila Parishads, Panchayat Samities, Gram Panchayats etc. has not enabled SC/ST people to stand on equal footing with others in rural areas. *Regarding reservation in services and educational institutions, there is no time limit.* However, there is no reservation of jobs for SC/ST in the Private Sector. It should be remembered that fruits of reservation policy are being taken away by a very small section of elites belonging to SC/ST. A majority of SC/ST is ignorant about their rights, due to illiteracy.

Opponents of reservation policy argue that it has not only aggravated caste tensions within the backward communities but also created a new class of oppressors. In Tamilnadu, Brahmans and other forward castes traditionaliy considered as oppressors of SC/ST, have already been replaced by others. In Bihar, it is not so much the Brahmans; the Rajputs and the Bhumihars who oppress the Scheduled Castes. According to them, it is the backward low castes like Yadavs and Kurmis who oppress the SC. They also hold that as a result of reservation policy, more and more castes press for inclusion in the Backward Class list. In Tamilnadu itself, the number of castes/subcastes listed as 'Backward' exceeds 200! Recently Vanniyar challenge to the DMK Government has brought into sharp focus the question—Is reservation an effective solution to the problem of social and economic backwardness? Reservation is not a measure which can possibly solve the problem of backwardness which is a by-product of economic backwardness. Indignities inflicted by upper castes on lower caste and Untouchables will continue unless the latter rise in revolt against the former. By legislation, untouchability has been made illegal but the practice still continues unabated in rural areas. Reservation policy is a sort of protective measure without which the downtrodden SC/ST and OBCs cannot have any hope for improving their lot. *It is a palliative not a curative measure.*

The replacement of old oppressors by new oppressors is not in any way related to the reservation policy. In the economic field, the middle peasants in rural areas have improved their status and many of them have turned into moneylenders who constitute the worst oppressors of poor SC/ST and OBCs.

It is obligatory on the part of the Government to protect and provide adventitious aids for the handicapped citizens and who can doubt that SC/ST and OBCs have been rendered backward by the economic system reinforced by the unjust dictatorial caste system. The self-appointed dictators proclaimed themselves to be chosen by the 'creator' to act as the rulers of the Hindu society. Thus, opponents of reservation policy are either descendants of the 'dictators' or their agents. They represent only 15% of the entire population. ST, SC and OBC constitute 85%.

The SC/STs are themselves not averse to ending the reservation, which makes them unduly dependent on Government largesse, most of which does not in any case reach them. *Even after more than 40 years, 18 per cent quota for them in Government service remains unfilled,* while reserved jobs are regularly de-reserved with impunity.

Social Justice, Merit and Privilege:

In a 'democratic' state, equality before the law is the most precious right and in our Constitution this is enshrined in Article 14. The right is further elaborated and made specific in Article 15, 16 and 29. These Articles prohibit discrimination against any citizen on grounds of religion, race, caste, sex, language or place of birth, whether in respect of employment or admission to educational institution, or access to public places etc. However, the clause 4 under Article 16 of the Constitution empowered the State to reserve posts in favour of inadequately represented backward class citizens.

The first major challenge to the policy of reservation was posed in Madras by two Brahman candidates, one each for admission into medical and engineering colleges. Under an order issued by the Madras Government, all seats in medical and engineering colleges were distributed among 6 communities in a fixed ratio and candidates of various communities could compiete only among themselves for admission, and not with candidates from other communities. The two Brahman candidates challenged the G.O. as being violative of the Fundamental Rights under Article 29 (2) of the Constitution. The Supreme

Court struck down the G.O. on the ground that the classification was based on religion, race and caste, and thus it was violative of Article 29 (2). This decision of the Supreme Court had serious implications for backward communities and serious political agitation followed in its wake. *There was an Amendment of Article 15 by the addition of Clause (4), which reads*: "Nothing *in this Article or in clause (2) of the Article 29 shall prevent the State from making any special provision for the advancement of any socially and educationally backward classes of citizens or for Scheduled Castes and Scheduled Tribes*".

Regarding acceptance of the principle of *protective discrimination* (Reservation) as a measure of social justice, Justice K. Subba Rao pointed out: "In a limited sense, the right to social justice may be defined as the right of the weak, aged, destitute, poor, women and children and other under-privileged persons, to the protection of the State against the ruthless competition of life. It seeks to give the necessary *adventitious aids to the under-privileged* so that they may have the equal opportunity with the more advanced in the race of life. *It is the balance wheel between haves and have-nots*." In fact, humanness of a society is determined by the degree of protection it provides to its weaker handicapped and lessgifted members. Unless adventitious aids in the form of reservation are provided to the backward classes, it would be impossible to suggest that they have equal opportunities with the more advanced classes. This is the reason and justification for the demand of social justice that there should be reservation in employments and admission to institutions of higher education.

Dictates of social justice demand that merit and equality are not turned into a fetish and the element of privilege enjoyed by upper caste Hindus is duly recognised and discounted for when 'unequals' are made to run the same race. In the traditional Hindu society, social, educational and economic backwardness had been a direct consequence of caste status; further, various other types of backwardness flowed directly from this crippling handicap.

The policy of reservation is opposed by the advocates of merit, who find it unfair when a SC or ST student securing 45% marks gets admission into a medical college in preference to a student from the general quota obtaining 70% marks. The resentment is much greater when a lower ranked SC/ST candidate is selected in preference to a much higher ranked general quota counterpart to an All India Service. This sort of reaction is based on two considerations: First, meritorious candidate is left out and secondly, the nation is deprived of best talents. *Merit is an amalgam of native endowements and environmental privileges*; and in Hindu society, environmental privileges had always been and continues to be the exclusive monopoly of the upper castes, Brahmans in particular. Obviously *'merit' on the part of low caste and Scheduled Caste Hindus had been retarded by caste regulations.* So the question of merit should be viewed in proper perspective so that in the name of doing justice to meritorious students, the underprivilleged candidate with potential merit may not suffer.

Anti-Reservation Agitations

Even though reservation for SC and ST has been accepted by most of the States, Gujarat is one of the States that experienced long drawn anti-reservation agitations twice between 1980 and 1985. Both agitations were led by dominant section of the middle class belonging to upper and intermediate Hindu Castes. The government had conceded to the demands of agitationists thereby the economic interest of SC/ST, and OBC in general was undermined. The agitations had the backing of capitalist class with which they have strong ideological and political links. They control the media and the educational institutions and dominate the bureaucracy and the policemen who supported the agitations directly as well as indirectly by flouting the orders of the executive heads. The Government introduced reservations for political exigency to catch votes as well as to diffuse the rising aspirations of the deprived classes. There is neither any perspective nor desire to use the reservation as a device for social transformation even of a limitated nature within the existing system. *It has been reduced to a mere political gimmic for electoral purposes.* Events of Gujarat suggest that it is almost impossible to unite all the deprived castes for any mass struggle on caste line to protect their rights. Caste-based organisations should take note of it. The deprived castes are not only divided into high and low status groups but also continue to subscribe the Brahmanical ideology which was actively nourished and propagated by nationalist Hindu leaders particularly Gandhiji who being a Gujarati had a special influence on the middle class belonging to upper and intermediate castes.

Backwardness of the SC/ST and OBC in educational Status is revealed in the following facts: in1901, 35% Brahmans, 44% of Vanias against 1% Kolis and Kanbi's were literate. Only 30 as against 3306 Vanias out of a sample of one lakh were literate in English. By 1931, however, 31% Kanbis became literate. Caste stigma was so strong that *when a Vankar (weaver) boy was admitted to high school in Vadadora in 1915, upper caste teachers and students protested and went on strike.* The strike was withdrawn only when Maharaja of Baroda announced that all who opposed admission of low castes would be dismissed. The two anti-reservation agitations in Gujarat were essentially struggles within the middle class—between the upper and middle caste members on the one hand and the new low caste entrants on the other. In Gujarat, the middle class has grown in size disproportionate to the economic growth of the region. This resulted in a steep rise in educated unemployment and consequent expansion of the lumpen crowd in urban areas. The lumpens have social ties with middle class on the one hand and underworld on the other. Their services are used by politicians in electoral politics. Amongst them aspirations for the possession of conspicuous consumption items as status symbol are growing but most of them are unable to find the wherewithal to satisfy their aspira- They thus have a strong feeling of deprivations. This is felt most amongst the upper and middle caste members who dominate the middle class. *They are jealous about the new entrants from the traditionally low castes.* They are victims of reactionary forces such as caste, region, language and religion. The attitude of upper caste members of the middle class, in general, is 'we will give, but they (SC, ST and OBC) should not demand.' Even persons having a liberal and Gandhian outlook believe that the Harijans should not assert their rights, however, legitimate they may be. *This attitude is a legacy of Gandhiji's preaching.* Whatever evil perpetuates in the political field in our country is rooted in Gandhian philosophy characterised by traditionalism and class-collaboration. The modern revisionists strengthen this reactonary force by their words as well as deeds.

In the eyes of law, there is no caste distinction, so politically there is on bar to any office for the low castes and Untouchables. *Our target of attack on caste system should be mental outlook engendered by the system.*

There can be no abolition of caste or class unless the system of exploitation of man is abolished.

Anthropolagists consider caste as an extension of joint family, so abolition of caste involves doing away with the family as an economic unit also. Selfishness and greed are engendered by the system of private property and nurtured by the caste system. The greatest deficiency in Hindu religion consists of absence of a any concern for the neighbour. Whatever feeling for others is exhibited by a Hindu is confined to the members of his caste whom he may not know personally. Such mentality is not only not denounced; it is rather a matter of pride that one has feeling for the members of his caste or community. Such an attitude is not congenial to revolutionary outlook and it is in this context we should examine the question of caste. In the battle against the caste system the principal objective should be the *substitution of caste spirit by class consciousness.*

On the question of reservation of posts in employment and seats for admission in educational institutions, there is some misunderstanding. The principle of equality (opportunity and treatment) places the 'strong' and the 'weak' in the same footing in the race of life. It is an established, well-recognised dictum of social justice that there is equality only among equals. *To treat unequals as equals or to give equal opportunities to unequals is to perpetuate inequality.* It is only by giving special protection and privileges, in the form of reservation to the down-trodden low caste people and the Untouchables that we can enable the latter to resist exploitation, to a certain extent, by the strong upper caste rulers. Without reservation, the low caste/Untouchables will have no opportunity to get out of the quagmire of backwardness. *In a democratic set up, reservation for them is entirely just.*

As yet there are many Untouchables who have not been included in the categorgy of scheduled caste/tribes. The just demands of caste or tribe based organisations must be supported by all democratic political parties including the communist revolutionaries.

Measures of protective discrimination served as adventitious aids towards the SC and ST population but the problem of backwardness towards the SC and ST in terms of economic social and educational status remained without appreciable improvement. In fact, the government was forced to adopt these measures in order to reconciliate the growing class contradiction between the upper castes and Untouchables organised under the leadership of Dr. Ambedkar. *The real motive was to create a class of privileged among the SC and ST people who would serve as collaborators of the ruling class.* In practice, this is what has happened. From the point of view of the government, these opportunities have played a significant role; an impression is created in the mind of some SC/ST people that the government is their real friend and they should limit their struggle within the confines of bourgeois Constitution. This is how, the challenge from the most exploited section of Indian population is counteracted. The section of SC/ST who succeed in availing of these privileges are automatically alienated from the overwhelming majority who are manual workers, illiterate and even ignorant about these aids. Thus, in effect, these palliatives strengthen the hands of upper caste exploiters. Babu Jagjivan Ram with his eminent position in the leadership and governments of both Congress and Janata Party could do little or nothing to improve the living condition of Scheduled Caste or Untouchable population.

As an election gimmick, Rajiv Gandhi announced on 9th August 1989, that there would be reservation of seats in local bodies for SC/ST in proportion to their population. In Tripura State, there will be 20 Assembly seats reserved for tribal population!

The study of Anthropology has made us aware of the mass of unfounded beliefs that influenced the lives of uncivilised human beings. Disease is attributed to sorcery, failure of crops to angry gods and earthquake to sin of the population. Human sacrifice is thought to promote fertility of the soil; bathing in holy water to wash away all sins! The life of the savage is hemmed by taboos and the consequences of infringing a taboo are thought to be frightful. Some parts of this primitive ideas died out in some parts of the world. Science, as a dominant factor in determining the beliefs of educated being only 300 years old and effective only in the West there is no wonder that in India the taboo of 'caste' persisted for 3000 years and even now influences the minds of Hindus, more in rural areas There had been a good number of celebrities in our country who considered infringement of caste taboo as a frightfully dangerous adventure!

Science has been the chief agent in dispelling primitive superstitions. In our country, during the last 200 years, none of the social reformers had anything to do with science and in the educational system there had been no attempt to cultivate scientific outlook. The result was the maintenance and perpetuation of the most retrogressive social structure of caste division. Gandhiji – 'Mahatma' and 'Father of the Nation' did not utter a word even indirectly criticising the evil consequence of caste system. *Dr. Ambedkar was probably right to say that Gandhiji did not speak against caste system because he knew that he would lose his leadership if he does that.*

To fight against caste is to fight for scientific outlook.

In view of the recent widespread anti-reservation movement of upper caste Hindu youth leading to even self-immolation, it is worthwhile to restate the magnitude of the problem of backwardness and deprivation of the scheduled caste, scheduled tribe and other backward classes (OBC).

With regard to the OBC's, it is universally recognised that after the transfer of political power in 1947, they benefited the most from the first phase of land reforms. Following the green revolution, the OBC's could dislodge the uppercaste Hindus from the dominant position economically as well as politically. The OBC's began to share with the upper castes the functions of arbiters and protector of Hinduism. However it must be borne in mind that it is *only a very small section of OBC's* which could be in this privileged position. The overwhelming majority of the OBC's continue to be marginal farmers, landless agricultural labourers, industrial workers or still in their traditional *caste occupations* and are victims of upper caste tyranny.

The relation between the OBC's and upper caste Hindus is fairly complex. Though compulsions of economic and political developments have brought them together, the process of accommodation is not without friction. In recent years the increase in reservation for OBC's has been the sources of tension between the OBC's and upper castes. Acceptance of Mandal

Commission Recommendations by the Janata Dal government gave rise to the vehement opposition from the upper caste Hindus in North India. The upper caste Hindus were already reluctant to treat the OBC's as social equals and resented encroachment by the latter in areas of their pre-eminence. Grant of reservation to OBC's in central government jobs is virtually dereservation of the monopoly of the upper caste Hindus in this arena.

Despite the Reservation Policy of the Government of India towards the SC and ST people, the situation vis-a-vis the number of SC and ST in higher posts, as compared to that during British rule in not much changed. For example, between 1882 and 1904, out of 16 ICS Indians, 15 were Brahmans; between 1969 and 1978 only 10 SC and ST candidates could qualify on merit in the IAS and IPS.

Regarding the world of high Government officers' post, the problem is far more challenging in the field of education; literacy percentages are as follows:

Year	*People in general*	*SC*	*ST*
1961	23.93	10.11	8.06
1971	29.48	14.54	10.89
1981	36.28	21.38	16.35

Evidently, the gap in literacy rates of SC/ST and general population is not changed significantly.

Unemployment figures, even that are doled out by the government, are more eloquent. At the end of 1950, the number of job seekers registered with employment exchanges was 3 lakhs, in 1971, the number rose to 51 lakhs, in 1981 to 1 crore 64 lakhs, and in January, 1989 to 3 crores 2 lakhs! Reservation policy of the Government of India is of little consequence to the problem of unemployment even amongst SC, ST and OBC population. *Janata Dal government approved of reservation in jobs but not in education*! Very recently, Mira Kumar had complained that many jobs reserved for SC and ST remain unfilled. *In China Mao Tsetung reserved seats in higher technical education, not in employment*! And the reservation was: workers' children 40%, Peasants' 40%, Soldiers' 10%, the rest 10%.

Even B.P. Mandal who recommended 27% reservation for OBC's in education and employment had stated that the reservation would not solve the problem of backwardness but reservation in higher administrative posts would enthuse the OBC's that their men are in the administration. Despite the existence of Untouchability (Offences) Act, Dalits are suffering the following privations as reported in Times of India. September 3, 1991. "Dalits are being denied entry into 80 percent of the temples in Marathwada . . . *Dalits are not allowed to enter temples in 75 of these 95 villages*. In Osmanabad out of 37 villages surveyed, Dalits are denied entry in temples in 22 villages . . . untouchability is still practised in most of Marathwada where Dalits comprising around 20% of the population. In almost half the villages surveyed, *the water facilities of Dalits and the upper canstes are separate . . . Dalits are not allowed to enter the houses of upper castes* in 81 of 95 villages . . . *Dalits were given tea by hoteliers in separate cups*. In six villages in Beed, *the barbers refused to cut the hair of Dalits* for fear of social ostracisation . . . *the burial grounds of Dalits and upper castes are separate in every village surveyed* . . . the Mahars and the Mangs are still condemned to doing the lowly, and allegedly polluting occupations like scavenging and removing carcasses , . . Dalits are ill-treated during ceremonies and functions. At weddings in 70 of the villages, they are fed on the streets or in animal stables, after the upper castes had eaten; they are also not allowed to celebrate Ambedkar Jayanti peacefully . . . In 24 villages, *Dalit members are not called to attend panchayat meetings* . . . In Kohni village in Nanded, when the panchayat meeting is held in the village temple, the Dalit members have to remain outside the temple.

According to V.T. Rajsekhar, the editor of "Dalit Voice", Bangalore, "*The worst sufferers in democracy are the Backward castes who are torn into several jatis.* Though in every state the BC's are the single largest population, they get hardly any representation in the legislature and in the decision making executive. That even after 13 years, the BC's, forming over 35% of India's population (the single largest segment of India) are not able to get the Mandal Commission Report implemented proves that democracy is of no use when it comes to numerically tiny sections. BC's do not constitute one single jati like Reddys, Jats, Marathas or Yadavs. They are a conglomerate of different jatis like barbers, gardeners, tailors and fishermen. For example, the Kurubas (shepherds) are Karnataka's single biggest jati like the Ezhavas of Kerala. But the Kurubas have no caste consciousness. And the upper castes have been fooling them continuously by idolising Kanakadasa whose very name suggests that he was a 'dasa' (slave) of the Brahminical social order (BSO) which killed their caste consciousness and annexed them into the BSO and thus enslave them. In the Hindi belt, Yadavas have been suffering the same fate like the Kurubas. The BSO promoted a Yadava tribal leader called Krishna a god-head and annexed this powerful cow-rearing jati into the BSO. But the continuous upper caste atrocities on them and Dr. R.M. Lohia's philosophy made the Yadava's revolt against the BSO and today they are a power to be reckoned with in the cowbelt. (Hindusthan Times, April 29, 1992).

Thus, fight for the continuation of reservations to the SC, ST and the OBC in education and employment is absolutely just; the traditional barriers to social and political equality may be removed through such struggles.

Bankim Chandra Chattopadhyaya, author of Vande Mataram song upheld the principle of equality: "You may have been born in a high family but that is not because of any special merit on your part. The other man's birth in a low family also is not because of any fault of his, so, his rights to the good things (comforts) of life are the same as yours. Do not come in the way of his enjoying them. *Remember he also is your brother-your equal.*" (Samya written in 1879). The status of the family is determined by the caste in which one is born! The gross inequality institutionalised in the caste system is nothing but crime against humanity.

Excerpts from 'Disputed Passages': A Report on Law, Reservations and Agitations-PUDR, Delhi, December, 1990:

"Who are the Backward Classes? Whether described as 'Socially and educationally backward classes' or as the 'backward Classes of citizens', the expression was intended to cover many more groups that are called under the category.

At the root of this diversity are the social relations of property, production and exchange as they evolved in historical time. *Caste in our social history served as the principal determinant of mechanisms of production of goods and services, distributian of resources and delineation of power. It was also the principal theoretical justification for inequitous social structure.* The Constitution is certainly an attempt to deny juridical sanction to this theoretical justification. But in reality post-colonial economy strengthened caste-based social structures and even reproduced them in modern sectors.

And in general we can find a broad correlation between the four tier hierarchial division of government services with some sort of caste hierarchy where the class I is filled with upper castes and class IV with lower castes. More strikingly we can find such correlations in the manufacturing sectors also.

Caste structure, thus strengthened and reproduced by contemporary political economy, is further consolidated by the arithmatic of vote blocks and the endless permutations and combinations of electoral alliances. Thus caste, still remains, to a considerable extent, a determinant of production, exchange and power, which in turn shaped the diversity and heterogeneity of the wide ranging, social groups that fall under the rubric of 'backward castes'.

One of the most eduring arguments against reservations is that it denies opportunities to meritorious candidates. This argument is based on one crucial assumption that marks scored by the students are the only unique measurement of his or her merit . . . *It ignores all other attributes like honesty, integrity and commitment.*

About 4-5 lakh students appear for preliminary IAS examination every year. The number of students selected is determined by the number of vacancies notified by various ministries and departments of the Central Government. The preliminaries have two papers; a compulsory General Studies Paper and one out of 22 optional papers offered. The number of candidates selected at subsequent stages from each subject is in direct proportion to the number who offered it as their option. Thus if 50% of students offer history and a further 20% offer sociology. then 50% of the next stage are reserved for history students and 20% for sociology and so on.

Thus, in the present system, a history candidate say with 45% would be selected over and above candidates who score say 75% from the less popular optionals like Physics, Engineering, Economics. And this meritorious history candidate thus selected (perhaps with a special interest in Ancient India?) over all other students, is expected (or is believed) to contribute to the efficiency of, say, the departments of Customs or Industry! . . . Even the most liberal estimates put the proportion of upper castes in the Central Government at not less than 65%. *The class I 'Officers' Assoclation of Central Goverment came out against reservations including for SCs and STs in clear violation of the Constitutional provisions that they are paid to enforce!*

TABLE 1

Deaths and Disturbances in the Anti-Reservation Agitation (August—November, 1990)

	North and West	*Police Firings*		*Caste Conflict*		*Suicides*	
		Number	*Killed*	*Places*	*Killed*	*Attempts*	*Deaths*
1.	Bihar	5	3	12	39	8	3
2.	Chandigarh	2	—	—	—	19	8
3.	Delhi	4	5	—	—	20	9
4.	Gujarat	2	2	—	—	5	—
5.	Haryana	11	4	2	2	36	24
6.	Himachal Pradesh	3	7	—	—	11	8
7.	Jammu	1	1	—	—	4	1
8.	Madhya Pradesh	—	—	—	—	18	11
9.	Punjab	1	1	1	—	29	23
10.	Rajasthan	4	—	—	—	4	2
11.	Uttar Pradesh	6	8	3	7	43	20

12.	Andhra Pradesh	—	—	—	—	2	1
13.	Karnataka	—	—	—	—	1	1
14.	Tamilnadu	—	—	—	—	1	0
15.	Maharastra	—	—	—	—	1	1
16.	Kerala	—	—	—	—	0	0
17.	Orissa	4	7	—	—	—	—
18.	All Others	—	—	—	—	—	—
	Total	43	38	17	38	202	112

Note : In 1982 when DMK leader Karunanidhi was arrested 5 committed self-immolation. MGR's illness in 1984 caused 12 self-immolation and his death in 1986, 26 suicides! In our country, rate of suicide in a year is 144 (recently).

TABLE II

Reservations in State Government Jobs (Percentage of Quota)

State/Region	*BCs (MBCs)*	*Women*	*EBCs*	*SGs*	*SCs*	*STs*	*Total*
1. Andhra Pradesh	25	Nil	6	Nil	15	6	52
2. Tamilnadu	32	Nil	Nil	20	18 (for both)		68
3. Karnataka	35	Nil	Nil	15	15	3	68
4. Kerala	40	Nil	Nil	—	8	2	50
5. Pondichery	NA	Nil	Nil	NA	16+	7.5	23.5
6. Maharastra	10	Nil	Nil	27	13	7.0	57
7. U.P.	15	Nil	Nil	15	30+	2	50
8. Bihar	8(12)	3	3	Nil	14	10	50
9. Punjab	5	Nil	Nil	–	25	Nil	30
10. Haryana	5	Nil	Nil	--	20	Nil	25
11. Himachal Pradesh	5	Nil	Nil	–	22+	7.5	34.5
12. J and K	42	Nil	Nil	–	8	2	52
13. Madhya Pradesh	?	Nil	Nil	–	16+	20+	36
14. Delhi	Nil	Nil	Nil	Nil	16+	7.5+	23.55
15. Gujrat	10	Nil	Nil	Nil	7	14	31
16. Rajasthan	Nil	Nil	Nil	Nil	16	12	28
17. West Bengal	Nil	Nil	Nil	Nil	15	5	20
18. Orissa	Nil	Nil	Nil	Nil	15	23	38
19. Assam	Nil	Nil	Nil	Nil	11	15	22

MBC = More Backward Caste
EBC = Economically Backward Caste
SG = Special Group.

The SC/ST communities, which had 22,5% reservations, had secured only 2.0% share in the jobs evcn after 4 decals of implementation of the reservations scheme.

TABLE 3

Occupational Distribution of Different Caste groups among Hindu Rural Households : (in Millions)

Occupation Agriculture	*Upper caste*	*Middle caste*	*Lower caste*	*Scheduled caste*	*Total*
Farmer	1.09 (24.38)	0.93 (7.57)	1.69 (6.95)	0.18 (1.54)	3.89 (7.35)
Cultivator	1.96 (43.91)	6.52 (53.30)	10.20 (41.79)	3.19 (27.05)	21.87 (41.35)
Share-cropper	0.17 (3.91)	0.76 (6.18)	1.51 (6.17)	1.00 (8.50)	3.44 (6.50)
Agricultural labourer	0.05 (1.09)	1.46 (11.91)	4.11 (16.85)	4.27 (36.19)	9.89 (18.70)
Forestry, Fishery and Livestock	0.02 (0.62)	0.17 (1.39)	0.81 (3.31)	0.28 (2.38)	1.28 (2.42)
Total Agriculture	8.29 (73.91)	9.84 (80.35)	18.32 (3.31)	8.92 (75.66)	45.37 (76.33)
Others	1.17 (26.09)	2.39 (19.65)	6.09 (24.93)	2.87 (24.34)	12.52 (23.42)
Total	4.46 (100.00)	12.23 (100.00)	24.47 (100.00)	11.79 (100.00)	52.81 (100.00)

Figures in brackets represent percentages of All India average. (EPW, February, 1979, Annual Number)

Constitutional Provisions Concerning Scheduled Castes

14. *Equality before Law.* The State shall not delay to any person equality before the law or the equal protection of the laws within the territory of India.

15. *Prohibition of discrimination on grounds of religion, race, caste, sex or place of birth.* (1) The State shall not discriminate against any citizen on grounds only of religion, race, caste, sex, place of birth or any of them.

(2) No Citizen shall, on grounds only of religion, race, caste, sex, place of birth or any of them, be subject to any disability, liability, restriction or condition with regard to—

(a) access to shops, public restaurants, hotels and places of public entertainment; or

(b) the use of wells, tanks, bathing ghats, roads and places of public resort maintained wholly or partly out of State funds or dedicated to the use of the general public.

(3) Nothing in this article shall prevent the State from making any special provision for women and children.

*[(4) Nothing in this article or in clause (2) of article 29 shall prevent the State from making any special provision for the advancement of any socially and educationally backward classes of citizens or for the Scheduled Castes and the Scheduled Tribes.]

16. *Equality of opportunity in matters of public employment.* (1) There shall be equality of opportunity for all citizens in matters relating to employment or appointment to any office under the State.

(2) No citizen shall, on grounds only of religion, race, caste, sex, descent, place of birth, residence or any of them, be

*Added by the Constitution (First Amendment) Act, 1951 S. 2.

ineligible for, or discriminated against in respect of, any employment or office under the State.

(3) Nothing in this article shail prevent Parliament from making any law prescribing in regard to a class or classes of employment or appointment to an office, (under the Government of, or any local or other authority within, a State or Union territory, any requirement as to residence within that State or Union territory) prior to such employment or appointment.

(4) Nothing in this article shall prevent the State from making any provision for the reservation of appointments or posts in favour of any backward class of citizens which, in the opinion of the State is not adequately represented in the services under the State.

(5) Nothing in this article shall affect the operation of any law which provides that the incumbent of an office in connection with the affairs of any religious or denominational institution or any member of the governing body thereof shall be a person professing a particular religion or belonging to a particular denomination.

17. *Abolition of Untouchability.* "Untouchability" is abolished and its practice in any form is forbidden. The enforcement of any disability arising out of "Untouchability" shall be an *offence pnnishable in accordance with law.*

46. *Promotion of educational and economic interests of Scheduled Castes, Scheduled Tribes and other weaker sections.* The State shall promote with special care the educational and economic interests of the weaker sections of the people, and, in particular, of the Scheduled Castes and the Scheduled Tribes and shall protect them from social injustice and all forms of exploitation.

1. Subs. by the Constitution (Seventh Amendment) Act, 1955, S. 29 Sch.

330. *Reservation of seats for Scheduled Castes and Scheduled Tribes in the House of the People.* (1) Seats shall be reserved in the House of the People of—

(a) the Scheduled Castes;

(b) the Scheduled Tribes[2] except the Scheduled Tribes—

(i) in the tribal areas of Assam;

(ii) in Nagaland;

(iii) in Meghalaya;

(iv) in Arunachal Pradesh;

(v) in Mizoram; and

(e) the Scheduled Tribes in the autonomous districts of Assam.

(2) The number of seats reserved in any State or Union territory for the Scheduled Castes or the Scheduled Tribes under clause (1) shall bear, as nearly as may be the same proportion to the total number of seats allotted to that State or Union territory in the House of the People as the population of the Scheduled Castes in the State or Union territory or of the Scheduled Tribes in the State or Union territory or part of the State or Union territory. as the case may be in respect of which seats are so reserved, bears to the total population of the State or Union territory.

(3) [3]Notwithstanding anything contained in clause (2), the number of seats reserved in the House of the People for the Schedule Tribes in the autonomous districts of Assam shall bear to the total number of seats allotted to that State a proportion not less than the population of the Scheduled Tribes in the said autonomous districts bears to the total population of the State.

2. Snbs. by the Constitution (Thirty-first Amendment) Act, 1974, S.3 for certain words.

3. Ins. by the Constitution (Thirty-first Amendment) Act, 1973, S. 3.

[4]*Explanation.* In this article and in article 332, the expression "population" means the population as ascertained at the last preceding census of which the relevant figures have been published.

Provided that the reference in this Explanation to the last preceding census of which the relevant figures have been published shall, until the relevant figures for the first census taken after the year 2000 have published, be construed as a reference to the 1971 census.

[5]332. *Reservation of seats for Scheduled Castes aud Scheduled Tribes in the Legislative Assemblies of the States.* Seats shall be reserved for the Scheduled Cates and the Scheduled Tribes (except the Scheduled Tribes in the tribal areas of Assam, in Nagaland, in Meghalaya), in the [6]Legislative Assembly of every State.

(2) Seats shall be reserved also for the autonomous districts in the Legislative Assembly of the State of Assam.

(3) The number of seats reserved for the Scheduled Castes or the Scheduled Tribes in the Legislative Assembly of any State under clause (1) shall bear, as nearly as may be the same proportion to the total number of seats in the Assembly as the population of the Scheduled Castes in the State or of the Scheduled Tribes in the State or part of the State, as the case may be, in respect of which seats are so reserved, bears to the total population of the State.

(4) The number of seats reserved for an autonomous district in the Legislative Assembly of the State of Assam shall bear to

4. Ins. by the Constitution (Forty-second Amendment) Act, 1976, S. 47 (w.e.f. 3-1-1977)
5. Arts 331 and 332 shall not apply to the State of Jammu and Kashmir.
6. Subs. by the Constitution (Thirty-first Amendment) Act, 1973, S. 4.

the total number of seats in that Assembly a portion not less than the population of the districts bears to the total population of the State.

(5) The constituencies for the seats reserved for any autonomous district of Assam shall not comprise any area outside that district.[7]

(6) No person who is not a member of Scheduled Tribes of any autonomous district of the State of Assam shall be eligible for election to the Legislative Assembly of the State from any constituency of that district.[8]

334. *Reservation of seats and special representation to cease after forty years.* Notwithstanding anything in the foregoing provisions of this Part, the provisions of this Constitution relating to—

(a) the reservation of seats for the Scheduled Castes and the Scheduled Tribes in the House of the People and in the Legislative Assemblies of the States; and

(b) the representation of the Anglo-Indian community in the House of the People and in the Legislative Assemblies of the State by nomination, shall cease to have effect on the expiration of a period[9] of (forty years) from the commencement of this Constitution.

Provided that nothing in the article shall affect any representation in the House of the People or in the Legislative Assembly of a State until the dissolution of the then existing House or Assembly, as the case may be.

7. Certain words omitted by the North-Eastern Areas (Reorganisation) Act, 1971 (81 1971), S. 71 (w.e.f. 21-1-1972)
8. Certain words omitted by the North-Eastern Areas (Reorganisation) Act, 1971 (81 1971), S. 71 (w.e.f. 21-1-1972)
9. Subs. by the Constitution (Forty-fifth Amendment) Act. 1980 S. 2 for "thirty years", (w.e.f. 25th January, 1980)

335. *Claims of Scheduled Castes and Scheduled Tribes to Services and posts.* The claims of the members of the Scheduled Castes and the Scheduled Tribes shall be taken into consideration; consistently with the maintenance of efficiency of administration, in the making of appointments to services and posts in connection with the affairs of the Union or of a State.

338. *Special Officer for Scheduled Castes, Scheduled Tribes, etc.* (1) There shall be a Special Officer for the Scheduled Castes and Scheduled Tribes to be appointed by the President.

(2) It shall be the duty of the Special Officer to investigate all matters relating to the safeguards provided for the Scheduled Castes and Scheduled Tribes under this Constitution and report to the President upon the working of those safeguards at such intervals as the President may direct, and the President shall cause all such reports to be laid before each House of Parliament.

(3) In this article references to the Scheduled Castes and Scheduled Tribes shall be construed as including references to such other backward classes as the President may, on receipt of the report of a Commission appointed under clause (1) of article 340, by order specify and also to the Anglo-Indian community.

340. *Appointment of a Commission to invesigate the clause of backward classes.* (1) The President may by order appoint a Commission consisting of such persons as he thinks fit to investigate the conditions of socially and educationally backward classes within the territory of India and the difficulties under which they labour and make recommendations as to the steps that should be taken by the Union or any State to remove such difficulties and to improve their condition and as to the grants that should be made for the purpose by the Union or any State and the conditions subject to which such grants should be made, and the order appointing such Commission shall define the procedure to be followed by the Commission.

(2) A Commission so appointed shall investigate the matters referred to them and present to the President a report setting out the facts as found by them and making such recommendations as they think proper.

(3) The President shall cause a copy of the report so presented together with a memorandum explaining the action taken thereon to be laid before each House of Parliament.

341. *Scheduled Castes.* (1) The President may with respect to any State or Union territory and where it is a State after consultation with the Governor thereof, by public notification, specify the castes, races or tribes or parts of or groups within castes, races or tribes which shall for the purposes of this Constitution be deemed to be Scheduled Castes in relation to that State or Union territory, as the case may be.

(2) Parliament may by law include in or exclude from the list of Scheduled Castes specified in a notification issued under clause (1) any caste, race or tribe or part of or group within any caste, race or tribe, but save as aforesaid a notification issued under the said clause shall not be varied by any subsequent notification.

13

Conclusion

The institution of caste is a social superstructure that had been built by the ancient political leaders on the economic base of primitive mode of production in a society already stratified into two classes: the exploiters and the exploited. Obviously, it is the class (position in the economic system), not the caste or social strata (occupation) that is primarily responsible for miseries in the material conditions of life and the consequent moral or ethical degradation. Caste-division had been designed and operated as an instrument to perpetuate class stratification. For Hindu society, caste is the single, most important cause of social, educational and economic backwardness. It acts as the greatest hindrance to class unity essential for liberation of the exploited toiling masses.

The existence of several million Untouchables is proof that the Hindu society is past-master in certain aspects of fascism. *Nowhere in history has there been such an enormous concentration camp with neither sentries nor barbed wire but only ideological subjection as sufficient fencing*. However, the fencing had not been effective always; the entire Muslim population of

Bangladesh, 80-89% of Christians, and Neo-Buddhists of our country did come out of the camp.

In Hindu religious texts like the Rig Veda and the Geeta it has been claimed that the Varna-division is a divine categorisation of human society aimed at the well-being of the human race as a whole. In this context the varna or caste is inseparable from Hinduism or Brahmanism. But in reality, the stratification of the society into castes is a matter of social significance with no religious implication. In fact, caste divisions, as they exist now, are very much against the basic Hindu doctrines of all-pervading Brahma. Actually, some of the scriptures do not accept the concept of caste distinction. For example, Bharadwaj, a disciple of Bhrigu argues (in Mahabharata): "If different colours indicate different castes, then all castes are mixed castes. We all seem to be affected by desire, anger, fear, worry, hunger, labour; how do we have caste differences then?" The story of Satyakama, the son of Jabala in 'Chhandogya Upanishad' clearly indicates that caste was looked upon as a matter of mental proclivity rather than of birth attribute. Nevertheless, the caste became hereditary since the last twenty centuries.

The orthodox Hindu holds that caste system is an integral part of Hinduism and he quotes supportive statements from religious texts. However, in Mahabharata, Yudhistira defined 'Brahma' in terms of behaviour (truthfulness, forgiveness, kindness etc.) and pointed out that an individual should not be considered a 'Brahman' just because he is born in a Brahman family, in case he lacks qualification nor need one to be considered a Shudra even though his parents were Shudras, The best argument against the acceptance of the caste distinctions is found in 'Bhavisya Purana' (Brahma Parva, 41, 45) "Since the members of all the four castes are children of God, they all belong to the same caste. All human beings have the same father and children of the same father can not have different castes". Nevertheless, quotations from religious texts can not eradicate or even tone down the baneful effects of caste-stratification. Pandit Iswar

Chandra Vidyasagar sought to achieve the introduction of widow remarriage by similar method but failed. Dr. B.R. Ambedkar the most prominent leader of Untouchables severely criticised Shastras and publicly clamoured for banning them. He even went to the length of actually burning 'Manu Samhita'. *According to him, caste distinctions can uot be abolished without destruction of belief in Shastras*. But belief in Shastras is something not susceptible to demolition by means of arguments or agitation. However, the political action of class struggle is the only way to bring about the abolition of the caste system and the spirit associated with it.

Abolition of classes is a very long protracted process. Mao Tsetung held that it will take not only decades but centuries for the completion of socialist construction i.e. abolition of classes. Abolition of caste is all the more difficult because of the religious sanction and the influence of primitive taboos with traditionalism in the minds of Hindu population.

The scheduled caste and scheduled tribe people consider that the only way to break the monopoly of the upper caste gentry is for them to unite as one caste and fight for the preferential treatment from the government. It is argued that the handicapped caste people must first be brought on par with the advanced castes as regards education and other economic opportunities before one can talk of abolishing the caste system. Today, the Backward castes and Untouchables can rise high only by subjecting the upper castes to political pressure through their caste membership. In such a situation, the call for immediate abolition of caste system would be counter-productive. The opposition would come from the Untouchables and low castes themselves! However, it must be realised by the people of low castes, SC and ST that reservations in employments and educational institutions would be mere palliatives unless the root of backwardness is tackled. Bulk of agricultural labourers, poor peasants, artisans, unskilled workers-all belong to lower castes, SC and ST. Domination over them by the upper caste rich peasantry is exercised through an informal bondage created and imposed through money lending. So with out breaking the stranglehold of existing production relation and changing the ownership of the means of production, the dependence of low caste poor on the high caste rich shall inevitably continue unabated. The Mandal Commission also states" ... *a radical transformation of the existing production relation is the most important single step* that can be taken for the welfare and upliftment of all the backward classes". But the radical transformation can not be expected of the existing state apparatus; it is possible only by 'New Democratic Revolution' under the leadership of proletariat. It should, however, be remembered that even after successful revolution, caste would not spontaneously disappear or wither away. Only through repeated cultural revolutions can the caste system be demolished.

The obvious economic foundation of the caste system have always been recognised. The foundation of caste system is gradually becoming weaker as a result of introduction of monetary economy in rural areas and industrialisation in urban areas. In the current epoch, the occupations are not hereditary and reverence towards Brahmans seldom discernible, particularly among elites. But the outlook of backward caste people is not undergoing rational changes commensurate with the social and environmental changes. This is so due to the influence of conservative elders of Hindu society and that of caste-based organisations which all the time foment only caste-spirit.

There is still considerable confusion about the implication of caste system, not only among members of caste-based organisation but even among some activists owing allegiance to Marxism who consider the problem of caste to be more important than that of class or economic exploitation. *It is imperative rather mandatory to give primacy to class over caste; caste-spirit has to be eradicated and class-unity strengthened.*

The caste being a social institution, battle against it would be mainly in the cultural front. The doctrine of 'Rebirth' and

'Karma', the foundation of the caste system has to be the ideological target to fight against; this can be effectively done only through class struggle.

Through the institution of Caste, the distinction between the mental and manual workers had been made permanent. The distinction was further re-inforced through the system of education introduced by British imperialism. Contempt for manual labour became ingrained in the psyche of the intelligentsia who act as an unconscious agent of compradore bourgeoisie.

The original stratification into the 3 varnas signified the separation of the mental and the manual workers. The Vaisnyas were condemned or assigned to the task of land cultivation (manual labour) in order to create and yieid surplus produced for the maintenance of the upper two varnas—Kshatriyas and Brahmans. *The very fact that Kshatriyas had been differentiated as a separate warrior stratum signified the advance of the process of dissolution of the primitive communal system and the beginning of the social division of labour leading to the formation of classes.* In primitive communal system wars of aggression as well as defence were the common responsibility of all; so the separation of a group of people as Kshatriya varna virtually represented the creation of a ruling coercive force—an *embryonic from of state apparatus.*

Caste discriminations in the society have to be directly fought on their own grounds but subordinated to the overall confrontation on class lines. Class struggle must be the keylink in the struggle against the criminal system of social inequality based on heredity.

Even through there are more than 2000 castes and subcastes, with regard to the social, educational and economic status, all Hindus can be divided into two principal categories forward upper caste (Dviya) mental workers and backward low-caste/untouchable manual workers. *This relation between the two groups is an antagonistic contradicition.* One is the exploiter and the other exploited.

Elaborating the dialectical relation between the base and the superstructure, Engels (letter to Block, September 1890) pointed out that although economic condition (means and relations of production) is the base, the constituents of superstructure—*philosophical and religious ideas certainly influence the class struggle and in many cases the latter play the cardinal role in determining the character of the htstorical process.* Apart from class contradictions, there are many other contradictions arising out of different forms of social inequality based on sex, race, tribe etc. and caste stratification is the worst of all because it is sanctified by scriptural texts. In our country replacement of slave system by feudal system had been effected through—an evolutionary process rather than a revolutionary upheaval of slaves under the leadership of feudal lords; the society retained many remnants of the slave system and the primitive, pre-Aryan taboo of purity and pollution was institutionalised as the caste system.

The ruling class always harps on "unity in diversity" in our country but the reality is just the reverse. Indian society, Hindu society in particular is characterised by disunity based on caste stratification. Moreover, there is no Indian in India; every one of us is either an Assamese, Bengali, Bihari, Oriya, Marathi, Gujarati, Tamil, Telegu and Malayalee. Apart from these two kinds of diversions based on caste and language, the principal contradiction is between the exploiters and the exploited-mental workers and manual workers. There are two more contradictions such as that between the old feudal landlords and the newly emerging rich peasants and that among the exploiting classes themselves. These three contradictions find manifestation according to castes/subcaste as (1) between the upper castes and lower castes/ Untouchable; (2) between upper castes and intermediate castes; (3) among the upper castes themselves. The contradiction between the Scheduled Caste Mahar population and upper caste Hindus of Maharashtra (mainly Brahmans) is basically a contradiction between the exploiter and the exploited. In Bihar, the contradiction between Brahmans, Rajputs and Bhumihars on one side and Yadavs, Kurmis, Kueris on the other is of second type. Amongst the new Kulaks that emerged as a result of capitalist development in agricultural production mention may be made of Mudaliars and Chettiars among Tamils, Rajus and Naidus among Telegus, and Nayyars among Malayalees. The contradiction between Kshatriyas and Patidars of Gujarat is of third type.

British rulers not only created the class of-Zamindar's on the model of feudal lords but also a new class of merchants, highly placed government executives and military officers. They all acted as agents of British imperialism and they were mostly upper caste Hindus. Some of the low caste/untouchable peasants migrated from rural areas to urban areas and became factory workers, domestic servants, office peon, coolies at railway stations and petty vendors of milk, vegetables and fruits. The class of traders and merchants newly emerging during British rule are Kshetris and Auroras in Punjab, Komat in Andhra Pradesh, Chettiars in Tamilnadu and Patidars in Gujarat. They joined the upper caste in the economic exploitation and social political oppression of Shudras and Untouchables.

More than forty years after the establishment of national government the position of the low caste/Untouchables in regard to economic and political status remains basically unaltered. Without a revolutionary change in economic base, no real change can be made in the caste system. Communists were the first to assert that the foundation of caste system lies in the production relation but they never carried out struggle against the criminal caste system of discrimination based on birth as a part of class struggle in the ideological and political front. Consequently leadership of the caste-based organisations could alienate the low caste/untouchable section of the exploited class from the influence of Communist Party.

There can be no progess towards abolition of caste system by carrying out class struggle without giving importance to the problem of backwardness between castes. Similarly, struggle against caste system can never succeed without relevant class struggle.

The caste system had been so successful that it inhibited the rise of merchants to the power in the State; it nipped capitalist accumulation in the bud. Consequently, there had been no development of modern technology till recently. The development of technology is closely bound up with the rise of the merchant class to power. It is the merchants, not the king or feudal lords, who financed research in order to develop new forms of production and trade. In China there are four strata according to occupation: Shih (scholar-gentry), Nung (farmer), Kung (artisans) and Shang (merchants). In India, the position of the merchants is third but that of farmers fourth or the bottom. T*he Communist movement in China very easily became based on peasantry who ranked second in social hierarchy*; whereas the Indian Communists depended more on middle class of urban areas; the peasantry ranking lowest in social hierarchy remained neglected till 1946. The healthy trend of 1946-48 was destroyed by the Trotskyite deviation led by BTR.

The religious prejudice of caste is so closely associated with class that its abloition is possible only through elimination of class division of the society. Lenin cautioned: "It would be stupid to think that, in a society based on the endless oppression and coarsening of the worker masses, religious prejudices could be dispelled by purely propaganda methods". (Collected works, Vol. 10, p. 83). He also pointed out: "*No educational book can eradicate religion from the minds of masses who are crushed by capitalist labour and who are at the mercy of the blind destructive forces of capitalism, until these masses themselves learn to fight this root of religion, fight the rule of capital in all its forms, in a united, organised, planned and conscious way. Does this mean that educational books are harmful or unnecessary? No, nothing of the kind. It means that Social Democracy's atheist propaganda must be subordinated to its basic task—the development of class struggle of the exploited masses against the exploiters*" (Collected Works, Vol. 15 p. 402).